"In *What You Really Need to Lead*, Rob Kaplan makes a breakthrough case for leaders to embrace an ownership model. This requires a mind shift in thinking and practice but provides the potential to unlock remarkable results. This practical but radical book is a clarion call to anyone leading a complex organization today."

—**DARREN WALKER,** President, Ford Foundation

"Rob Kaplan's brilliant third book on leadership is his best yet. He challenges all leaders to think like owners, thus bringing that deep sense of responsibility and enterprise perspective to organizations large and small. Reading Kaplan's book is like having a wise mentor at your side. All leaders can benefit enormously from his wisdom and advice."

—**BILL GEORGE,** professor, Harvard Business School; former CEO, Medtronic; and author, *Discover Your True North*

"Every organization, whether business, governmental, or philanthropic, should insist that its entire leadership team read this book cover to cover. It is written with wisdom, punch, and color. Only Rob Kaplan, with his own leadership experience at Goldman Sachs, his mentorship of students at Harvard, and the unusual pace and clarity of his words as an author, could have delivered such a masterpiece about leadership."

—**WILLIAM H. DRAPER III,** cofounder and cochairman, Draper Richards Kaplan Foundation

"Building a highly functioning and committed team requires opening oneself up—being vulnerable—and allowing empathy, support, and discussion to permeate. Rob Kaplan offers concrete steps for how to achieve this leadership feat. Follow his advice and you'll undoubtedly become a stronger leader."

> —**R. C. BUFORD,** President of Sports Franchises and
> San Antonio Spurs General Manager, Spurs Sports &
> Entertainment

"*What You Really Need to Lead* offers a fresh view of what leadership means, as well as compelling, real-life stories and practical advice for both aspiring and seasoned leaders. If you're wondering how to lead and make a positive difference in the world, read this book and start today."

> —**BARBARA BUSH,** cofounder and CEO,
> Global Health Corps

"*What You Really Need to Lead* is honest, direct, and filled with practical advice. I found it especially useful as an entrepreneur trying to build a culture of ownership in my growing team. It helped me understand how I could do more—and *be* more—by focusing on a few very tangible steps that made me a better leader."

> —**ZAMEER KASSAM,** CEO and Chief Designer,
> Zameer Kassam Fine Jewelry

"*What You Really Need to Lead* provides you with the rational evidence for introspection as a leader and empowers you to take responsibility for your actions, strengths, and weaknesses, and to understand your influence on your team. It will set you on a course for success by helping you define your and your business's value."

> —**VANESSA KERRY,** cofounder and CEO, Seed Global Health; Associate Director of Partnerships, Center for Global Health, Massachusetts General Hospital; faculty, Harvard Medical School

WHAT YOU REALLY NEED TO LEAD

WHAT YOU REALLY NEED TO LEAD

The POWER *of* THINKING *and* ACTING LIKE AN OWNER

ROBERT STEVEN KAPLAN

Harvard Business Review Press
Boston, Massachusetts

Kaplan, Robert Steven.
    What you really need to lead : the power of thinking and acting like an owner / Robert Steven Kaplan.
       pages cm
       ISBN 978-1-63369-055-4 (hardback)
1. Leadership.   2. Executive ability.   I. Title
    HD57.7.K36633 2015
    658.4'092—dc23

ISBN: 9781633690554
eISBN: 9781633690561

To my son, Michael

Contents

Contents

WHAT
YOU
REALLY
NEED
TO
LEAD

Demystifying Leadership

What It Really Means, How It Can Be Learned, and Why Ownership Is Essential

Leadership. It's one of the most important and frequently discussed subjects in our society. Consider these views on leadership from a selection of iconic historical figures and influential thinkers:

> *It is better to lead from behind and to put others in front, especially when you celebrate victory when nice things occur. You take the front line when there is danger. Then people will appreciate your leadership.* —NELSON MANDELA

> *A genuine leader is not a searcher for consensus but a molder of consensus.* —MARTIN LUTHER KING JR.

A leader is one who knows the way, goes the way, and shows the way. —JOHN C. MAXWELL

A leader is best when people barely know he exists, when his work is done, his aim fulfilled, they will say: we did it ourselves. —LAO TZU

Management is doing things right; leadership is doing the right things. —PETER DRUCKER

———————

What is *your* definition of leadership?

How does this definition help you figure out what to do if you:

- Face a challenge in managing an individual, a team, or an entire company?

- See an issue in your community and wonder whether you should take steps to do something about it?

- Observe a colleague struggling with a particular task and consider whether you should offer to help?

- Notice a piece of trash on the floor at work and consider whether you should bend down and pick it up?

What does it really mean—to *you*—to be a leader?

———————

Leadership touches every aspect of our lives. We regularly talk about the need for leadership in our communities, institutions, companies, and at all levels of government. We often lament a lack of leadership when things go wrong and wish we had more of it when organizations seem to drift. When things go right, we are quick to attribute the good outcomes to effective leadership.

Given all the various contexts in which we talk about leadership, the extensive scholarly work that has been done to explore its key elements, and the tremendous effort universities and companies have put into developing it, you would think we'd have a strong, shared understanding of what it is. In my experience, we do not.

Either You Have It or You Don't—Right?

These days, when I meet new people, I often tell them that I'm a professor at Harvard Business School. In response, people are typically complimentary, seem intrigued, and want to hear more. They usually follow up by asking me what I teach. "Leadership," I answer proudly. This answer is typically met with a blank stare or a skeptical frown. "I don't think you can teach that," or "I'm not sure that can be learned," they say. They explain that, in their view, you're either a leader or you're not. I respond by trying to explain how leadership can be taught. I tell them that I believe leadership skills can be—and often have to be—learned.

By and large, the people I speak with—many of whom are CEOs or aspiring executives—don't buy it. They argue that leadership is an innate quality or a state of being. Either you have it or you don't. They believe that there is an elite group of people who possess certain qualities, and another less talented group who simply don't. As a consequence, they think that trying to teach leadership is likely to be a futile effort.

This reaction used to really upset and frustrate me. Why couldn't I convince people that leadership is a capability that can be cultivated and learned? I have seen it done over and over again, including in my own executive experience.

Can Leadership Be Learned?

Through several decades, scholars and practitioners have done an extensive amount of work to help people learn to be leaders. This work has delineated key elements of leadership, identified critical challenges that leaders face, and even suggested various approaches for how leadership qualities can be developed (see appendix B for a leadership reading list). Additionally, over the last fifty years, tens of thousands of students have attended classes at leading universities or taken part in company-sponsored leadership development programs—all designed to cultivate and improve their leadership abilities.

Despite this abundance of excellent thinking, training, and advice, many people continue to believe that leadership can't be learned. They often use expressions such as "born leader" or "natural leader." These expressions implicitly equate natural personality traits—such as charisma or extroversion—with leadership skills. Based on my own experience, innate traits don't necessarily translate into effective leadership. And conversely, the lack of certain traits doesn't preclude someone from becoming a superb leader.

For several years, I have tried to demystify leadership to make it more accessible to practitioners. I have taught classes, studied the writings of various leadership scholars and successful practitioners, led and worked on various business projects, and engaged with business and nonprofit leaders in an effort to help them improve their performance. During this time, I have written two books designed to help people develop their leadership capabilities as well as to better understand themselves. My goal was to provide useful guides that could be put into practice and help people more effectively build their careers, run their organizations, and reach their unique potential.

However, the more I have worked with executives and aspiring leaders, the more I have realized that a central reason why so many people struggle with the question of whether leadership can be learned—and whether they are themselves leaders—is that "leadership" means something different to each of us. Whether we're aware of it or not, each of us has a different conception of what leadership is and what a leader does.

Our own individual conception, whatever its origins, can have a powerful impact on our actions. I have found that many talented people—including some of those who have used my previous books—are still hampered in their development because of their mind-set and implicit assumptions regarding the nature of leadership.

What Does Leadership Really Mean—to You?

Conceptions of leadership in our society are shaped in very specific ways. For example, many people get their frame of reference from those larger-than-life characters celebrated by popular culture, and especially by television and the movies. Think of John Wayne, iconic tough guy in his many film roles, commanding firefighters, Green Berets, and the cavalry. Somehow we just know that Colonel Mike Kirby—Wayne's character in *The Green Berets*—didn't need to learn to lead. He had a charismatic personality and was blessed with great natural instincts, which helped him *figure out what to do*. In these films, we really don't get any insight into how he developed his abilities. We're left to assume that he must have been born with an acute sense of timing and an innate ability to understand and command people.

Many people base their conceptions of leadership on their knowledge of prominent figures past and present. For example, think of political leaders like Franklin Roosevelt, Ronald Reagan, Angela Merkel, or Winston Churchill. Or think of business pioneers like Sam Walton, Estée Lauder, or Steve Jobs. Alternatively, think of sports figures who led their teams to a championship. We tend to form some type of narrative regarding what made them great; they were captivating speakers, or highly innovative in a way that changed an industry, or brave under pressure and performed in the clutch. How they arrived there isn't completely clear to us. Our image of them is often frozen in time at the point of their greatest achievement.

In addition to popular culture and prominent historical figures, our conceptions of leadership are shaped by people we know directly: teachers, family members, bosses, or prominent local leaders in our communities. The styles of these leaders can vary enormously. They might be distinctive personalities—confident and charismatic. They may seem to possess special qualities that help them have an impact on people and shape events. These special qualities may seem to be developed and built on innate gifts, in the same way someone has athletic ability or musical talent. Watching them may lead us to think that either people have these gifts or they don't.

If the leaders we admire are really successful, they might be celebrated on the covers of important magazines or in headlines on the web. If and when things subsequently go wrong—sometimes only a short time later—these same leaders are often vilified just as enthusiastically as they were praised. When that happens, people who used them as their role models feel disillusioned and are forced to rethink their conceptions of leadership.

What's Your Definition of Leadership?

A few years ago, I started asking senior executives to write down their definitions of leadership. I have learned a lot from the responses. The definitions varied widely. Some would say that a leader inspires and mobilizes others to advance a shared purpose or accomplish a specific set of strategic objectives. Some respondents say that leaders have a knack for thinking about the future and being in the forefront of some trend or movement—a cause, a new way of thinking, or an innovative approach to solving a problem—and then convincing and rallying others to go along with them. They cite intellectual curiosity, vision, positive energy, charisma, and communication skills as critical elements of leadership.

Still others say that getting people to follow your lead is an outdated notion and that today, leadership is more about empowering and serving others. They believe that a leader creates the conditions and environment that enable people to be innovative and take action.

I agree with elements of each of these definitions, and yet, each seems incomplete.

Then there are the more "practical" and "savvy" executives who have a very different conception of leadership. They think all this touchy-feely, qualitative stuff is basically irrelevant. They argue that scholarly studies of leadership are interesting, but for the most part, don't ultimately matter very much. Their analysis goes more or less as follows: "Just tell me one thing—is the leader running a business that is making money? If the business is making money, then the person running it must be a good leader. If the business isn't making money, then the person running it probably isn't a good leader. That's leadership—results!"

By this definition, leaders and leadership practices can come and go, depending on the fortunes of their firms and their industries. Based on this idea of leadership, they believe that first and foremost, leaders should spend their time worrying about revenues and profits. The qualitative stuff might help, but there's no substitute for generating good commercial results.

This conception may strike you as unduly narrow because of its single-minded focus on results. You may even think that it is an exaggeration of a particular point of view. However, the reality is that many of us consciously or subconsciously evaluate leaders exactly this way: by *results*. Leaders look a whole lot smarter and more competent when things go well. Did you win reelection? Then you must be an effective government official. Does your team have a winning record? Then you must be a good coach. Did you accomplish the military mission? If yes, then you must be a strong commander. Is your company making a lot of money this year? Then you must be a skilled executive.

The problem with the single-minded results orientation is that it can be heavily affected by factors that are outside the control of the executive. In other words, it helps to pick the right industry, benefit from a strong economy, and maybe have a little luck. These external factors may distract a leader from proactively focusing on those practices and issues that are under their control and would help them build a more sustainable enterprise. The history of business is replete with stories about executives who were celebrated as superb leaders, only to be cast aside as abject failures when their businesses began to lose money or even failed.

How could a person go from being a great leader to a bum within a few short years or even a matter of months? Is leadership that fleeting or fragile? That's a scary thought. If it's true, why would anyone step up to a challenging leadership situation in which the odds of success appear to be low?

In Search of a Shared Understanding

After several years of these discussions, I finally had an unsettling epiphany: we really don't have a widely shared understanding of what leadership is. But how could that be? There's a whole industry (of which I'm a part) that focuses on leadership and, in my opinion, has collectively done superb work in unpacking the key elements of leadership.

In appendix B of this book, I include a detailed list of important and influential writings on leadership authored by selected academics and practitioners. Companies have drawn extensively on this body of work, investing heavily in training, teaching, and career-development processes to build leaders in their organizations.

In my own executive career, I have benefited greatly from reading much of this work, which emanated both from academia and from the executive suite. Yet, despite all this, there still seems to be confusion about the subject of leadership.

Does this confusion matter? Yes, because if you're confused about what a leader is supposed to do, it's probably going to be harder to figure out what *you* should do when you get into a leadership situation.

The Issue

I have come to believe that when all is said and done, we are often better at teaching leadership best practices than we are at addressing and resolving the various conflicting conceptions of leadership. A person's conception of leadership matters because it will likely have a strong influence on how he or she processes the writings, leadership coaching, and development practices he or she experiences. We may have underestimated the enormous power of various conflicting conceptions. That power can work against us, in that it undermines our ability to get to a widely shared understanding of leadership.

This lack of shared understanding is a big problem— for all of us. We often talk about the need for more and better leadership in the world. Many of the ills of our society are explained by a lack of leadership. Most of us want to be effective leaders. Most CEOs say that the biggest thing their organization lacks is leadership.

But what, exactly, do we want more of? Very often, we can't precisely say, or we disagree on what we want—but we can all agree that we want more of it!

If we can't agree on a clear definition of leadership, how do we decide whom to hire and promote? How do we recognize a leader when we see one—for example, how can we tell whether a candidate running for office will be an effective leader? More importantly, what exactly are we supposed to do when we get into a leadership position?

To answer this, we usually fall back to our own preconceptions, or what we've seen previous bosses do or how our current boss behaves. We may even solicit advice from others inside or outside our organizations. Very often, though, this advice is contradictory because advisers we consult have their own unique ideas regarding what a leader does.

As a result, we may flounder and improvise. What would my boss want me to do? We might revert back to company practices, or what we've done in the past that worked, or maybe look to what others are doing in a similar situation. When we're presented with a situation we haven't seen before, we may just go with our instincts. This isn't necessarily a bad approach, unless you're part of a team or a company where individual members each take their own path in a given situation, which can result in disorganization or even chaos.

Wouldn't it be helpful if we had a better shared understanding of the key elements of what a leader does and how that applies to us, individually, in our current jobs and in our daily lives? Is there a framing that would help organize all the great advice and best practices that seem to help individuals and organizations be more effective?

With this enhanced understanding, we could take actions that would fit our industry, our company, and our own individual characteristics.

Creating a Leadership Frame: It Starts with an Ownership Mind-Set

I have spent the past several years trying to demystify and define "leadership." Building on my own experience as well as the work of numerous scholars and practitioners, I have tried to break leadership down into terms that are accessible and understandable. My purpose is to help people take actions that fit who they are and further their unique aspirations and those of their organizations.

In this book, I will offer a framing for your leadership journey. I will make the argument that leadership starts with an ownership mind-set. That is, do you think as if you are in the shoes of a decision maker and act in a manner that takes ownership of the consequences of your actions? Do you focus on adding value to others? Do you take responsibility for the impact of your actions on others—both positive and negative? Do you take responsibility for continually learning to become a leader and learning to understand yourself? As you will see throughout this book, the concepts of leadership and ownership are tightly intertwined.

Once you have developed an ownership mind-set and are willing to take responsibility for learning to be a leader, you will improve your effectiveness by empowering others to act in the same way. This book will discuss techniques for engaging others in a way that helps you dramatically improve your leadership. It will also suggest actions you can take that will help get you started on the road to becoming a better leader.

I hope that this framing will help you create a clearer mind-set for your activities, provide tools and techniques that you can use today, and help you realize that *you* can be a leader. My purpose is to discourage your inclination to wait to be a leader someday or leave leadership to someone else. My goal is to convince you that you can and should strive to think like an owner and be a leader today—*now*—as well as tomorrow and into the future.

This book comprises five chapters:

Chapter 1—The Ownership Mind-Set. What does it mean to be a leader? What does it mean to have an ownership mind-set? In this chapter, I will explore the critical elements of leadership and pose several key questions you must ask in your quest to become a leader. Some of these questions deal with intellectual issues, while others address emotional issues.

Exploring these questions will likely confirm some of your existing instincts about leadership and cause you to rethink some of your assumptions. It may reinforce some of your theories that grow out of past experiences. It should help you make your instincts and theories much more actionable. At the same time, you will likely find that you've been a leader more often than you thought, but that you've also failed to act like a leader in certain critical situations, which may explain some of your current regrets.

We don't often get "do-overs" in the real world. But learning from the past and considering what you could have done differently can be a highly productive exercise for adapting your behavior and shaping your future.

This chapter should help you realize that you have it within your power *today* to make a significant difference in your company, family, and community. Leadership isn't reserved for presidents, generals, and

CEOs—the "big shots." You don't need a written invitation to be a leader. It is a mind-set and way of behaving that begins today.

Chapter 2—Tackling the Challenges of Leadership. If your reaction to the discussion in chapter 1 is, "Well, what's so hard about that?!" this chapter provides a good antidote. Being a leader is often challenging, and frequently people fail because they haven't developed the capacity to play that role, particularly as the role evolves. Being open to learning, resisting the dangers of isolation, and accepting some level of vulnerability are critical elements of sustainable leadership.

Many people aren't yet "in shape" to perform the actions that will help them to assert themselves and make an impact. Or they have been successful for a period of time, but then something changes and they don't have the capacity to adapt to the new situation. In this chapter, we will explore several of the reasons why people so often fail to lead or ultimately lose their way, and we will look at some of the tools you can use to combat these challenges. First among these tools is your ability to be confident enough to ask questions and listen to others. You'll see that leadership is less frequently about ability, or power, or even resources. Far more often, it is about your mind-set and your ability to adequately understand your situation and yourself.

Interestingly, leadership failure can occur even though those around you see you, the situation, and what needs to be done remarkably clearly—even as you are blind to it. In this chapter, we'll discuss the pitfalls of leadership and actions you can take to address your blind spots, recognize transitions more clearly, and make failure far less likely.

Chapter 3—Mastering the Essential Processes of Leadership. This chapter sets forth a regimen of steps for learning to improve your leadership skills. Embedded in this book's conceptual framing of leadership is a detailed set of processes and habits that you will need to master in order to build your capacity to lead and then sustain that leadership. The first process is intellectual: articulating a clear vision, setting priorities, and creating alignment with your vision and priorities. The second process is far more amorphous and complex; it focuses on *understanding yourself.*

Although you may not be consciously aware of it, you are executing (or failing to execute) these processes every single day. It takes hard work and continuous attention to master these processes. Leadership is not a state of being or a destination where you finally arrive and can then relax. On the contrary, it is a journey that requires consistent diligence, focus, and attention. I believe these processes are very much analogous to getting in shape or losing weight. Just like these processes, if you let your efforts slide, your ability to exhibit leadership behaviors is very likely to atrophy.

This chapter will explore vision, priorities, and alignment processes, as well as your effort to better understand yourself. You may find that some of these activities are easier for you than others. Additionally, these efforts can be particularly challenging, because they are taking place in parallel. Lack of attention to one of these processes may make it harder to accomplish the other. This chapter will lay out a series of very specific questions you need to ask to continually develop your capacities for leadership.

Chapter 4—You Can't Do This Alone. Leadership is a team sport. That is to say, your success is inextricably linked to the activities and contributions of others. You are highly unlikely to become a leader or develop your leadership capabilities all by yourself. Almost certainly, the steps described in this book will be far more difficult to master if you don't improve your ability to cultivate relationships and work effectively with others. Do you have relationships based on mutual understanding, trust, and respect? Are you able to reveal information about yourself in relationships? Do you have friends or colleagues who will tell you things you may not want to hear, but need to hear?

In this chapter, I will discuss the importance of relationships in leadership development. I will also suggest a number of steps you can take to cultivate effective relationships and describe techniques for improving your ability to build more effective bonds with others. If you can begin to master this skill, you will find that everything else in this book will be much easier to accomplish.

Chapter 5—The Ownership Path as a Lifelong Journey. If you are beginning to believe that following the steps in this book will help you to pursue a more fulfilling path in your life, what do you want to do about it? What tools and techniques can you use that will help you jump-start your efforts? How might you want to try these tools? Where do you start?

This chapter is intended to get you moving down the path. It will help you start the journey from where you are today. It begins with helping you explore what you truly care about. What would give more meaning to your life? What are your skills and passions? What is your own definition of success? Are you living your own dream or someone else's? What actions do you want to take to reach your unique potential?

The world is full of challenges and opportunities. This chapter will outline several ideas for how to think about your next moves and offer various alternatives for making the most of your abilities. It will discuss intrinsic versus extrinsic motivators and ways to get a better grip on how they apply to you. This chapter will help stimulate your thinking about how you might put your toe, or foot, or entire leg in the water.

The key elements of the preceding five chapters are summarized in Appendix A: Essentials of What You Really Need to Lead. This visual guide should prove useful as a framework and a training reference for the concepts in this book.

Getting Started

My goal in this book is to create a framing that will convince you that *you* can be a leader. The book is also intended to give you a framework for developing your leadership habits and substantially improving your leadership skills.

In particular, I will stress the importance of developing an ownership mind-set and a willingness to keep learning. I will also discuss a range of issues and suggest a number of specific actions that will help you see the world more clearly and determine your own role in making a difference. At its core, this book is intended to make leadership accessible—*today and into your future.*

As discussed, leadership doesn't require a written invitation. It isn't something that only "important people" can do. It isn't a function of money, power, or title, although these elements can certainly affect, for better or worse, your ability to pursue your aspirations. Leadership isn't something you do later or reserve for an elusive "someday" when you reach a certain age, or have more skills, or wield more power.

Leadership is a way of thinking that engages your special talents *now* and, ideally, for the rest of your life. It involves a process of learning and being open to adapting your behaviors. It is something you need to work at versus a state of being or a destination.

The progress of the world very much depends on your willingness to engage in this activity. This progress will require addressing issues we see today as well as developing the capacity to address issues we can't currently even begin to imagine. Whatever the case, the world's problems aren't going to be solved by "someone else" over the next few decades. They will be addressed—or won't be—depending on what *you—and people like you*—do. What's it going to be?

The world needs your leadership.

Suggested Follow-Up Steps

- *Write down your definition of leadership. What are the key elements?*

- *What forces do you believe have shaped your definition—for example, do your role models come from popular culture, parents, previous bosses, teachers, or public figures? What key assumptions do you make in coming up with your definition of leadership (for example, you have to be an extrovert to be a leader, leadership requires charisma, you need formal authority to be a leader, and so on)?*

- *How is this definition helping or hindering your ability to be a leader today? How might it be holding you back?*

- *What steps will you take to continue learning and improving your leadership skills?*

CHAPTER ONE

The Ownership Mind-Set

*The Power of Thinking and
Acting Like an Owner*

Leadership is about what you do. It is not a position you hold or a state of being. Your leadership potential is certainly shaped by who you are as a person and your life experience, but whether this potential is realized depends on what actions you take.

Sometimes your actions will lead to positive outcomes, and sometimes they will lead to negative outcomes. While external factors can influence outcomes—making money, setting profit records, winning elections, securing a piece of business, and so on—these outcomes typically are the result of a sustained period of high-quality actions.

The point is that results, by themselves, don't define good leadership. Instead, good results typically occur as a result of good leadership.

Years of effective leadership usually precede sustainably good results. By the same token, good current results can often mask poor leadership, although this may not become apparent for several years, sometimes too late to prevent real damage.

An Ownership Mind-Set

If effective leadership typically precedes sustainably good results, what are the key elements that tend to be critical to effective leadership? If there is a wide range of potentially effective leadership styles, do these styles share certain key features? In my experience, the answer is yes.

Effective leadership begins with having the right mind-set; in particular, it begins with having an ownership mind-set. This means a willingness to put oneself in the shoes of a decision maker and think through all of the considerations that the decision maker must factor into his or her thinking and actions.

Having an ownership mind-set is essential to developing into an effective leader. By the same token, the absence of an ownership mind-set often explains why certain people with great promise ultimately fail to reach their leadership potential.

An ownership mind-set involves three essential elements, which I will put in the form of questions:

- Can you figure out what you believe, *as if you were an owner*?

- Can you act on those beliefs?

- Do you act in a way that adds value to someone else: a customer, a client, a colleague, or a community? Do you take responsibility for the positive and negative impact of your actions on others?

These elements are not a function of your formal position in an organization. They are not a function of title, power, or wealth, although these factors can certainly be helpful in enabling you to act like an owner. These elements are about what you do. They are about taking ownership of your convictions, actions, and impact on others. In my experience, great organizations are made up of executives who focus specifically on these elements and work to empower their employees to think and act in this way.

In this chapter, we'll discuss the key essentials of an ownership mind-set and how they translate into effective leadership. We will also address how these concepts might relate to you and your life.

Do You Try to Figure Out What You Believe as If You Were in the Shoes of a Decision Maker?

The world is full of people with opinions. Television, radio, and other media are brimming over with commentators making suggestions and offering seemingly authoritative advice to government officials and corporate executives about what they ought to do. At dinners and cocktail parties—and around the water cooler at work—we talk about what others should do or should have done, or the flaws of our bosses. There's usually very little risk in this banter, and often no one even remembers what was actually said. It can be fun and sometimes interesting. On occasion, giving our opinions may make us feel better about ourselves, because we're weighing in on important issues. We may even think that by asserting our views, we are acting like leaders.

In our jobs, we may give our opinion on an issue from a functional or departmental point of view—in other words, a limited perspective. Or we may give an opinion without fully thinking about the issues and weighing the interests of various constituencies that our boss has to consider in order to make an important decision. We may do this because we don't have access to additional information or, alternatively, because we believe that broadening our perspective simply isn't part of our job description.

This kind of opinion giving may be quite appropriate and adequate in any number of situations, but it doesn't constitute leadership. Leadership requires much more. It starts with taking on a broader perspective in figuring out what you truly believe should be done—that is, as if you were an owner.

I Thought I Did a Good Job

Jim, a vice president of a consumer goods company, called me to discuss a problem he was facing. He was a former student of mine and was calling to seek advice. He had just had a jarring experience, and he was trying to make sense of what had gone wrong.

Jim had been working on the launch of an important new product for his company. He was a key member of a multifunctional launch team that was headed by the senior vice president in charge of one of the company's key divisions. The team was charged with conceiving of all aspects of the new product's design, packaging, marketing, and distribution strategy. This product was vital to Jim's company, because the market share of several of its core products was eroding, and senior executives urgently needed to find new avenues for growth. They thought that this new product would address an important consumer need and reestablish the company's position in the minds of its customers.

Each member of the project team was assigned one aspect of the new product and its launch. Jim's responsibility was to focus on the point-of-sale promotion for the product. He felt this wasn't the most critical assignment, but—given the importance of this project and the high quality of the other team members—it was still a good opportunity.

After several weeks of work, he came up with a detailed plan regarding display and placement for the product within each retail context: grocery stores, drugstores, and other consumer outlets. In addition, he developed alternative point-of-sale materials to be used in some of the regional product tests that were about to be conducted.

During this period, the project team met once a week, with each member of the team reporting on his or her area of responsibility. The senior vice president wanted every team member to be aware of the plans for all aspects of the launch. He hoped that team members would question each other and learn about each other's assignments, and thereby produce a more effective launch strategy.

Initially, Jim was very pleased with his work on this project. "I thought I did a very good job," he told me. To come up with the detailed plan, Jim had assembled a subgroup comprising several of his subordinates. He felt great about how things were going, which was why what happened next was so disconcerting.

At one of the late-stage project team meetings, Jim was asked to present his final recommendations. To his surprise, several members of the project team roundly criticized his proposal. They felt it was out of step with the nature of the product, price point, and likely consumer buying behavior. In particular, the members of the larger team felt his point-of-sale positioning was more consistent with an impulse purchase, whereas they believed strongly that this product should be positioned and priced as much more of a premeditated buy on the part of the consumer.

Jim was shaken. After the meeting, the team leader took him aside and asked him how much he really understood about the product being launched. "I've been in every meeting," Jim replied, "and I've listened carefully." If that was true, the team leader asked, how could he be so out of step with the team members regarding the product's positioning? Jim countered that he thought he had responded well to what he had heard in the meetings, and that he had also drawn effectively upon his past experience working on other successful launches.

The team leader proceeded to ask Jim a series of specific questions: "Who do you think should buy this product? How should it be priced? How should it be packaged?" Jim admitted that he hadn't really thought about these issues because they weren't explicitly part of his specific assignment on this project. Other team members, he argued, were supposed to be worrying about *those* questions.

The team leader was exasperated by Jim's comments. Before ending the meeting, he gave Jim some pointed advice. He urged him to think about how he would answer these questions if he were the team leader, rather than simply a member of the team with a narrow set of specific responsibilities.

Jim thought this was an odd recommendation. He called me to get my reaction to what had happened and to ask for suggestions regarding how he should respond to the project manager's challenge. My reaction was straightforward: "Jim, your team leader has given you some great advice. I agree with him. Pretend that you're responsible for this situation. Really try to think as if you were the boss, or even owned the company. Imagine that your life depended on getting every aspect of this launch right. How would you do it? You're a talented guy. Think like an owner and use your talents to answer his questions."

Jim acknowledged he hadn't thought about this approach, in part because his current and previous bosses had never encouraged him to think or act this way.

"That's going to take a lot of thought and analysis on my part," he said, "and maybe even some serious soul-searching. Are you sure this is really my role? Do I really have to do all that?"

"Yes," I responded. "If you want to be a leader, you absolutely do."

He decided to take this challenge seriously. He interviewed other team members and applied his broad skills and talents to think through every aspect of the product positioning. He even conducted some of his own research at selected retail outlets, looking to see how competitive products were being positioned. After doing all this work, he began to realize that his initial recommendations were at best superficial, and at worst radically misaligned with what he now thought would work for this product launch.

He came to a disturbing insight: *he had done a lousy job.* He had not applied a leadership mind-set in his work on this project assignment. As a result, he had done inferior work and made himself look bad to others in the company. He decided to summon his courage and apologize to the team leader and the entire project team.

The project team members were gracious about his apology. They were impressed that he had had the guts to admit he was wrong, go back, and redo his work and rethink his recommendations. He proceeded to explain the new positioning recommendations, which his teammates quickly approved. He felt as if he had been welcomed back as a valued member of the team.

He realized that he had learned something valuable from this experience. This was reinforced when the senior vice president, who was widely recognized as a rising star in the company, told him, "From here on in, Jim, I hope you'll act like a leader in this company. You have great potential here, but only if you start thinking like an owner. Define your job broadly, rather than narrowly."

Jim promised himself that in the future, he wouldn't think like a narrow functionary, but instead approach his work as if he was an owner of the company. This new mind-set helped make his thinking much clearer and his work much more effective. He had a new prism for judging his thinking and his actions.

Developing Conviction

It sounds simple: "Think like an owner." In fact, it is hard to do. It requires you to put yourself in the shoes of the decision maker. You may realize that you prefer not to be in those shoes. There's too much pressure; there are too many considerations; there are too many constituencies. With all the complexity, constant change, and myriad of issues in the modern world, it may be easier to rationalize more narrow thinking: *Dammit, it's not my job!*

Yes, it is your job, if you want to be a leader. If it frustrates you, or makes you agonize, or even creates a heightened level of stress for you, then you need to get used to experiencing those feelings. The more you practice this, the better you'll get at doing it.

I would urge you to begin to *believe* and internalize the view that thinking like an owner is central to your effectiveness in your job. Thinking like an owner means getting to conviction. "Conviction" is meant to describe a threshold level beyond which you feel a high level of confidence about what you truly believe should be done.

Many leaders spend their lives striving to get to conviction about what they would do in a particular situation. The reality is that, much of the time, they may not have a strong point of view. They keep gathering information, agonizing, and assessing until they reach a threshold level of confidence.

On the other hand, some leaders need to be wary of getting to conviction too quickly, or having such a strong initial point of view that they fail to take into account key considerations that are crucial to making a good decision. Each of us has blind spots, may be prone to ideological points of view, or may be unaware of our own subtle biases. As a result, we each need to also take sufficient time to gather information, consider alternative arguments, agonize, and make sure we are arriving at a balanced judgment.

The point is that the process of searching for conviction can be very challenging. The contextual factors and considerations are changing all the time; competitors take significant actions; products get commoditized, and so on. In addition, different people looking at the same situation may come to different points of view about what should be done. To cope with all these factors, leaders need to perform analysis, seek advice and input from others, debate alternatives, and generally ruminate. Much of the time, this process may feel like a grind.

While you're going through this grind, you don't always need to know exactly what to do; you don't always need to have the answers. However, as a leader, you do need to be constantly striving to get to a level of conviction on key issues. How do you do this? You and your team need to focus your efforts on taking the necessary steps that will help get you to a sound judgment.

With practice, you will learn to understand yourself better and increasingly learn what conviction *feels like*. As you search for it, you will get better at gearing your efforts to work in a way that will help you get to that feeling. Leaders don't look for excuses for why they can't act like an owner. Instead, they embrace the challenge of ownership and encourage their teams to do the same. It helps if, as subordinates, they were regularly encouraged and empowered by their bosses to put themselves in the shoes of decision makers. "Superb professionals define their jobs broadly," one of my former bosses regularly said to me. "They are always thinking several levels up."

This may explain why many business schools, including Harvard, teach using the case method. This approach certainly can be used to teach analytical techniques, but, for me, it is primarily an exercise in learning to *get to conviction*. After you've studied all the facts of the case on your own, and after you've debated those facts in study groups before class and again in class, what do you believe? What would you do if you were in the shoes of the protagonist?

The case method attempts to simulate what leaders go through every day. Decision makers are confronted with a blizzard of facts: usually incomplete, often contradictory, and certainly confusing. With help from colleagues, they have to sort things out. Through the case method, students learn to put themselves in the shoes of the decision maker, imagine what that might feel like, and then work to figure out what they believe.

This mind-set is invaluable in the workplace. It forces you to use your broad range of skills. It guides you as to what additional analysis and work needs to be done to figure out a particular business challenge.

Leaders don't need to always have conviction, but they do need to learn to search for it. This process never ends. It is a way of thinking. Every day, as you are confronted with new and unexpected challenges, you need to search for conviction. You need to ask yourself: What do I believe? What would I do if I were a decision maker?

Aspiring leaders need to resist the temptation to make excuses, such as *I don't have enough power*, or *it's not my job*, or *nobody in the company cares what I think*, or *there just isn't time*. They must let those excuses go and put themselves mentally in the shoes of the decision maker. From that vantage point, they will start to get a better idea how it feels to bear the weight of ownership.

Practice Thinking as an Owner

Try this exercise. Think of all the pressures a CEO must face—taking into account the interests of stockholders, employees, customers, the general public, and regulators. He or she must also deal with competitive pressures and disruptive innovations in the market, as well as consider ethical, legal, and economic issues in weighing key decisions. Often these considerations create tensions that involve trading off various factors and balancing interests. Imagine yourself in his or her shoes. Think through how you would factor in each of these considerations. Consider how it feels to know that satisfying one constituency or addressing one consideration will likely cause some other constituency to be dissatisfied with your choice.

Practice performing this analysis in a variety of situations. How does this mind-set affect how you do your own job in the company? I think you will find that this approach and mental discipline will dramatically broaden your perspective and improve your insight, decision making, and overall effectiveness.

Think how many candidates for office describe what they would do if elected, and then, when they get into the job, back away from the promises they made as candidates. Why? We sometimes think that they have been dishonest or said what they thought they needed to say in order to get elected. Very often, though, it is simply the case that once they're actually sitting in the hot seat—the decision maker's seat—they begin to take into account all the critical factors that they had discounted or ignored when they were on the outside looking in. They begin to understand the emotional weight of sending troops to war, the unpopularity of raising taxes, the influence of various lobbying factions, and the discomfort of being unpopular with voters.

Thinking like an owner is rarely easy. But, if you start practicing this discipline today, you will get better and better at it until it becomes second nature. You will be better able to empathize with and respect the thinking of senior executives and counterparts. With practice, you will also begin to see the power of this approach in bringing out your very best.

The Ability to Act on Your Convictions

Once you've gotten to conviction on an issue, are you able to act?

Leadership, in small ways and in big ways, is about ultimately finding a way to act. There are lots of people who can figure out what they truly believe as if they were responsible, but still can't bring themselves to *do* something about it.

Why? There are lots of reasons why people fail to take action. Taking action involves taking some degree of risk. Each of us is wired differently, and certain types of actions have the potential to make each of us very uncomfortable.

We could fill up pages and pages of text describing the types of risks and fears that keep people from taking action. Some people are afraid to speak up, make waves, or upset their boss; some are afraid that they'll be wrong and look stupid; some are afraid that the boss will disagree and think less of them; others are afraid people won't like them; some people are afraid that taking action will stress them out so much that they won't be able to sleep at night.

Another reason people fail to act is that they aren't confident that they have sufficient skills or they're not sure they have thought through all the ramifications of their actions. They may believe that they don't yet have a plan of action that is credible, or they don't have the interpersonal and other skills needed to effectively persuade people to go along with and carry out that plan.

Alternatively, people may refrain from taking action because career, family, or hefty financial obligations magnify the risks of taking action. Maybe you just bought a new home, had a baby, or fear that an economic downturn may make your job prospects more tenuous. Maybe you're hoping for a near-term promotion and the stakes are simply too high for you to stick your neck out.

You get the idea. There is no shortage of reasons people can find not to act.

Leadership, though, is about ultimately finding a way to take action. Aspiring leaders learn that when they get to a high level of conviction, they have to find ways to push themselves to overcome their fears and reservations in order to speak up or take other appropriate action. They learn to manage their lives so as to mitigate risks that tend to keep them from acting—for example, they focus on saving their money and do their best to avoid getting financially overextended. They learn to go beyond *what* should be done to figuring out *how* it should be done. They learn to develop a thick skin so that if people disagree with them, they take it constructively rather than personally. They learn to engage in constructive debate. They focus on learning how to create an action plan.

This may be as simple as figuring out a strategy for speaking up to a senior person, or may be as complicated as thinking through multiple action steps from time zero to several weeks or months into the future. It may involve determining what resources are needed (human and otherwise), assessing what communication and coordination are necessary, and developing a systematic road map for each step. Sometimes the process of action planning is enormously helpful in illuminating the flaws in the original idea and leads to going back to the drawing board to develop a new or amended alternative. In this way, action planning feeds back into developing the concept of what should be done, as well as how it could be done.

All this takes practice. The more you do, the better you become. It can be made easier if the culture of your organization encourages people to take action. For example, it is enormously helpful if senior leaders model this behavior and explicitly encourage young colleagues to speak up, express their views, and take appropriate action, thereby empowering them to act on conviction.

Of course, taking action doesn't always work out as planned. In my own career, I have led teams that made decisions that turned out poorly. In the aftermath, after the bad outcomes had become apparent, there was almost always someone on the team who would approach me and say something to the effect of, "You know, I never agreed with that decision. I knew that decision would be a mistake." My first response was to ask something like, "Well, if that was the case, why the heck didn't you speak up?! You were in all the meetings. You agreed with all the decisions!"

Typically, he or she might respond by offering one excuse or another: "Well, it seemed like your mind was made up," or, "The group wouldn't have listened," or, "I didn't think I had the power to persuade people on the team," or, "I didn't think it was my role to challenge the rest of the team," and so on.

The world is full of smart people, some of whom have the ability to put themselves in the shoes of the decision maker and get to conviction about what they would do if they were in charge. In my experience, though, only a relatively small subset of that group has the skills and fortitude to step up and constructively *act*. It may not be pretty, and they may get beaten up for acting, but they know that, ultimately, translating conviction into action is essential to becoming a leader.

In No-Man's-Land

Henry, a senior executive in a large industrial corporation, did not like what he saw happening in the company. He had spent his entire career with the firm and felt that, in recent years, it had become excessively focused on quarterly profits, rather than serving the needs of the customer. Henry believed that in the past, when there was a trade-off decision to be made between investing in product quality or customer service and increasing profitability, the firm almost always thought long term and decided to forgo short-term gain in favor of longer-term franchise enhancement and longer-term profit.

A new CEO had been put in charge four years earlier. He had previously been the company's CFO, and Henry believed that he had subtly changed the emphasis of the company from profitably serving customers on a consistent basis to focusing on near-term profitability. Now, when trade-off decisions were debated, the dominant questions became, "What is most likely to help profitability this year, and how is it likely to impact the stock price?" To his increasing dismay, Henry observed that most of the other executives in the company went along with this shift, evidently because they wanted to stay on good terms with the new CEO. He felt angry with the new CEO, and he felt even angrier with his peers.

By the time he came to see me, Henry was discouraged and even depressed. He described the situation, while answering my occasional questions along the way. I asked him, "Have you spoken up? What does the CEO say in response to your concerns?"

Henry gave me a surprising answer: "I haven't expressed my concerns."

"What? Why not?" I asked.

Henry explained, "He won't listen to me! I don't have that great a relationship with him. If I upset the CEO, what am I going to do then?"

I asked him, "If you don't speak up, who will? Who has more power or influence than you do? Nothing is going to change if senior folks don't step up and lead."

I wish I could tell you that this story had a happy ending, but it didn't. Henry just couldn't summon up the courage to raise his concerns directly with the CEO. A year later, he told me that the CEO was seeking his opinion less frequently and was beginning to exclude him from important meetings. Henry felt marginalized and began thinking seriously about leaving the company.

Ironically, that same CEO came to visit me about a year later. (Due to confidentiality, I didn't disclose to him that I already knew another side of this story.) It was painful to hear *his* perspective: "The thing is, I have this senior executive, Henry, who has wilted since I became CEO. He is afraid to disagree with me and give me advice. I came in from the CFO role, and I really needed some of the marketing and manufacturing guys to step up and debate with me. I know I have a blind spot sometimes when it comes to financial issues versus long-term franchise choices. I agonize over these trade-offs every single day, but I can't do it alone. Henry has really disappointed me. He has broken to the downside as a leader. I am seriously looking at promoting one of his subordinates to replace him."

Ugh. By failing to act on his convictions, Henry actually put himself in no-man's-land. He thought he was pleasing the boss, but instead, the boss lost respect for him because he was not looking for a yes-man or -woman; he was looking for *leadership*.

I have rarely seen an executive damage his or her career by finding an appropriate way to act on a high level of conviction. I *have* seen numerous executives limit their effectiveness and impair their upward mobility by playing it safe and keeping quiet when they felt strongly about an issue at their firm. Each of us needs to figure out a way to act, even if it's scary and feels dangerous. It isn't necessary to totally dismiss our fears, but it is useful to weigh them against the risks of doing nothing. The zeal to act as an owner can help you overcome these legitimate hesitations.

What Helps You Step Up and Take Action?

What are you afraid of? Everyone has fears and insecurities. However, if you are a prisoner to these fears, you will be held back from making an impact and reaching your potential. If you fail to act on your convictions, it is highly unlikely that you will operate at your best.

How do you deal with these issues? I suggest that you try using various "mental models" that can help you see things more clearly and summon the strength to get over the hump, take some level of risk, and *act*.[1]

A mental model is an exercise that calls for relaxing a real (or imagined) constraint, thereby freeing your mind to see more clearly what should be done. For example:

- If you owned the company, would you be willing to act on your conviction? (This is an example of using the ownership mind-set we have discussed in this chapter.)

- If you were wealthy, what would you do?

- If you had only two years to live, what would you do?

These questions are intended to help you figure out what is holding you back from taking action and also come to grips with how your hesitancy may be undermining your development as a leader. If you are unduly cautious because you wish you could be more persuasive and charismatic when you speak, try speaking up on a topic about which you have strong convictions. I think you'll find that your own version of charisma will emerge when you speak up or otherwise take action on those issues about which you feel strongly. If you think you're boring and uninspiring, try changing your *approach*: learn to act when you have conviction on an issue.

A Focus on Adding Value

Leadership is ultimately about creating value that benefits someone else. This last element of leadership isn't discussed often enough or as seriously as it should be. Great leaders and great companies become great because they focus on adding value to a customer, a client, a community, or other key constituency. A failure to focus on adding value often explains why leaders and once great companies sometimes go off the rails. They lose sight of or get confused about *why* they are doing what they are doing. They stop taking ownership of the impact of their actions on others.

The concept of adding value is captured in a motto used by the Navy SEALs. The SEALs have a phrase that is hammered into them constantly during their incredibly rigorous training: *if you know the why, you'll figure out the how.*

Over the years, I have come across numerous executives who are good at figuring out what's good for *them*, and then acting on that. That may work for a while, but if that's as far as they go, this approach doesn't lead to sustainable success. If their actions do not create value for others, they aren't leading—at least according to my definition—and are unlikely to be doing their best work. Too many people today consider themselves "leaders" merely because they are in important positions. However, if their focus is not on how to benefit their key constituencies, the power of their position alone won't be enough to ultimately make them leaders. This helps explain why superb leaders evaluate their own success by their ability to help their team members become successful, as well as their ability to add value to key external constituencies.

Perhaps your reaction is to say that you thought that leadership was primarily about achieving results. As discussed earlier, good outcomes—such as making money—come as a result of adding value for a sustained period of time. Of course, there are many examples of people who have experienced short-term success without adding value to others, but ultimately, it's hard to find someone who has built a lasting success over a sustained period of time without an intense focus on adding value. Great businesses and business leaders know that profitability comes as a result of helping team members become successful, as well as adding distinctive value to customers over a prolonged period of time.

This mind-set also involves taking an appropriate amount of responsibility for the potential negative impacts of that business on key constituencies, including the general public. History is full of organizations that added value to some of their constituencies but directly or indirectly harmed others. An example would be a business that sells a product that benefits its customers but, at the same time, emits harmful pollutants that undermine the health and welfare of local communities. Leaders need to think broadly about adding value but also assessing and taking an appropriate degree of responsibility for mitigating the potential negative externalities of their operations.

The tough thing about adding value, and trying to mitigate negative impacts you might create, is that these objectives need to be revisited and updated on a regular basis. The world changes, industries change, societal norms change, competitors take actions, regulations change, and products and services get commoditized. As a result, how you add value has to be continually updated.

Disillusioned with Our Leaders

When we lose confidence in our leaders, it is often not because we have come to doubt their capabilities. No, more often, it is that we begin to doubt that they are thinking as owners and acting on conviction. In addition, we begin to believe that these leaders and their organizations are not really focused on adding value to their community or customers. When this happens, we gradually stop buying their products or refuse to vote for them on Election Day.

CEOs of companies can get so caught up in the pressures of delivering quarterly profits and meeting shorter-term shareholder expectations that they begin to speak more about "making the plan" than about "serving customers" or being a good corporate citizen that considers its impact on local communities. When this happens, it can create substantial confusion and concern in the minds of employees, customers, and the general public. It can send a message that what matters most is finding a way to make the numbers, rather than adding value to customers and more broadly to society. The emphasis on research and innovation may begin to slip. If this goes too far, customers may begin to sense that the company is becoming more impersonal and less focused on building a long-term relationship by serving their needs. Market share may begin to erode, as customers begin choosing alternative vendors that are more focused on adding value to them.

What Went Wrong?

Susan was the founder and head of a building-products distribution company, headquartered in the Midwest. She had previously been an employee of a larger multistate building-products company. In that role, she had first been a buyer, then ran a distribution center, and then became a regional manager. After several years, she began to dream about starting her own business. She developed a business plan, sought out investors, and opened her first distribution center, which served customers in a relatively small geographic area.

The business got off to a great start. Over several years, she expanded the firm's regional footprint by establishing additional centers in three new geographic areas. She secured several more rounds of equity financing to fund growth, and things continued to go well. In the company's eighth year of operations, however, it experienced its first down year, followed by a second down year. Susan knew that the company's problems were partly the result of an economic downturn and challenges related to weak residential construction trends. At the same time, she also began to question whether she had the right team of executives.

She came to see me to discuss the situation. She explained that she was upset and disappointed: "I'm furious with my team. Either they are incompetent, or they just don't care as much as I do about the business. I feel like I have the weight of the world on my shoulders, and my investors, who up to now have been so supportive, are starting to ask me challenging questions in our regular calls.

"I knew this was a cyclical business, but I thought we would adapt to the cycles much more effectively than we have. It's been much tougher than I expected. I thought running my own company was what I *wanted*," she sighed. "Sometimes I wonder what I could have been thinking, to want to do this."

I asked Susan how she was spending her time. She admitted that she wasn't sure. We pieced together how her activities had changed as the business expanded. She recalled that when she opened her first distribution center, she was in that location every day—talking with customers, making key purchasing decisions, and coaching her employees. As she opened the second, third, and fourth locations, though, she spent much less time with customers and with her people, and much more on managing investors, focusing on the balance sheet, and scouting out potential new locations.

After this warm-up, I asked her to tell me how the company added value to customers. She paused, and eventually responded, "That's an odd question. As a businessperson, I mainly focus on how to make money. That's what I talk to my people about—*we need to generate profit!* That's how you build a business, right?"

"Well, not exactly," I replied. "Great businesses and profitability come as a result of adding value. So let me ask you again: how do you add value? What's distinctive about what you do?"

Susan thought some more and gave me an answer that seemed to surprise her more than it surprised me. "You know," she said, "I guess that when I first started the business, I *was* obsessed with some version of your question. I talked to my customers—who were primarily building contractors and subcontractors—to understand their product and service needs, and based on what they told me, I picked merchandise, focused on new construction and remodeling trends, and created a game plan for making sure we had excellent customer service. It all seemed to work. But after that initial period, I guess I shifted gears to focus more on the financial aspects of building a business, because I thought that's what businesspeople are *supposed* to do. Certainly, most of the questions from my investors seem to be about revenues and profits."

I told her that I thought she was making a classic mistake that many entrepreneurs make. She had stopped focusing on what made the business great and started to excessively focus on ancillary issues that were important but ultimately not central to success. She needed to get back to focusing on how to add value. This was particularly challenging, given the cyclical nature of this business and resulting changes in consumer behavior.

Ultimately, she would find that her investors wanted her to focus on the drivers of the business, even though at any given moment, their questions were more focused on revenues and profits. Further, her people might not have been as bad as she thought. Instead, they were likely confused by her priorities—or lack of them. They didn't understand her vision for how the company added value. They weren't sure what they were supposed to be doing. All this confusion was heightened by the downturn in home construction and changes in the buying habits and service needs of her customers. These changes should have caused her to update her vision and key priorities for the business, so that her employees would know how to adapt to the more challenging environment.

In short, she was failing to lead.

Susan admitted that she hadn't fully connected adding value to customers with building a sustainable business. She certainly hadn't recognized that this is what it means to be a leader.

She went back to her company and did some soul-searching. She spent several weeks asking questions about how the company truly added value to customers. To do this, she spent more time talking with customers and her staff. She got reconnected to what was selling and what wasn't—and why. She soon concluded that the company was stocking the wrong merchandise for the needs of her core building-contractor customers. It was also clear to her that service had slipped. She made it her focus to reorient her merchandise buying, create ongoing processes to assess and reassess customer buying habits as well as building trends, and stress better customer service.

After several months, the company began to enjoy increased sales and profitability despite a challenging economic environment. Today, she looks back on those two years as a great learning experience. "I learned to keep my focus on adding value," she told me on the phone recently. "That's how I built the business in the first place, and it's how we'll succeed going forward. The focus on adding value clarifies our decision making and priorities, aligns our people, makes the business stronger, and makes me a much more effective leader. Sustainable results come as a consequence of our effective leadership actions."

Own It—Don't Wait for a Written Invitation

Figuring out what you believe as the decision maker, summoning the courage to act, and focusing on adding value to others—if these are the key elements of leadership, do you need to own a company or be in a senior position at a firm to be a leader? Do you need to have a certain type of job or title to exercise leadership? Do you have to be an owner, in order to think and act like an owner?

No, you do not. Leadership is mind-set and action dependent, not position dependent. You don't need to manage anyone to be a leader. Conversely, you can manage thousands of people and not be a leader at all. It all depends on what you *do!* Do you figure out what you believe as if you were an owner, and do you act on those beliefs? Do you focus on adding value to others?

You don't need to have a specific title, position, or equity stake in order to do this. *You don't need a written invitation.*

The Janitor as Leader

I met the principal of a grade school located in the northeastern United States. She told me a story about Carl, the janitor in her school. One day, a six-year-old child at the school wet his pants—not all that unusual, but with the potential to be very traumatic for the child. Carl observed that the child—standing in a hallway looking very upset—had had an accident. Carl took it upon himself to find the boy's teacher. Together, they took the child off to another room, helped him get cleaned up, somehow found him a change of clothes, helped him to calm down, and eventually sent him back to his regular classes. Their goal had been to help the child avoid the humiliation of being sent home, with all his classmates knowing that he wet his pants. Once the child was back in class, Carl resumed his normal janitorial duties of picking up trash, cleaning floors, and so on.

To me, this is a story about leadership. I don't know much else about Carl, but I can tell you that *he is a leader.*

He is probably the lowest-ranking person employed in that school, with the most menial title, yet he thought and acted like an owner in this situation. He could have observed the child's distress, decided that it wasn't his job to worry about it, and gone on with his duties. But no, he stopped, took responsibility, and did what he thought was best for the child and for the school.

He exhibited *leadership*. I'm pretty certain that the principal of that school is a leader, too, because she clearly created an environment in which Carl felt empowered to figure out what he believed and act on conviction, in a way that added value for a student.

This story is about as concise and powerful an example of thinking and acting like an owner—of leadership—as any I can think of. Leadership doesn't require a fancy job description. It's not something you hope you might get to engage in someday, if you ever get a promotion to a big job. Leadership is a way of thinking and acting that focuses on adding value to others—*when the opportunity arises*.

Great companies are built around people who act this way. In excellent organizations, these are the type of behaviors that get rewarded when executives consider whom to promote. This was certainly true for me, during my own career in business. Before I offered someone a leadership job, I looked for evidence that the person had already acted like a leader. If he or she hadn't exhibited leadership behaviors—helping others, thinking and acting like an owner, taking initiative, going above and beyond rather than limiting his or her actions to the explicit requirements of a job title—it was unlikely that a fancier job title was going to magically transform this person's mind-set and behavior.

Is There a Shortage of Leadership?

So often, people talk about a leadership crisis—an alarming shortage of leaders to handle all the problems in the world today. But is there really a crisis?

I have spent a good part of my life working with leaders. I love striving to be a leader, helping others become leaders, and helping leaders succeed. I see people from every walk of life and in geographies all over the world. Based on my definition of leadership, I believe that there is no shortage of leadership in this world. In fact, there are millions of leaders in every corner of the world and in every walk of life.

I think the reason we perceive a leadership crisis is because many of our more visible leaders—those with formal power and substantial titles, running bigger institutions—all too often fail to think and act like owners in the way we've discussed in this chapter.

How can this be? Why do people fail to act like leaders? Maybe they didn't know what they were supposed to do? Maybe they thought results were all that mattered? Maybe they used to act like owners, but the pressure of a high-stakes job made them become cautious and start thinking more tactically about short-term outcomes, rather than acting with conviction and with a focus on adding value to key constituencies?

The sometimes disappointing performance of executives in visible positions of power often causes us to think that we just don't have great leaders anymore. I disagree. We may simply be looking at the wrong indicators and in the wrong places. Having a big job doesn't ensure that a person will act like a leader. Leadership is a function of what you do versus your status or position.

There are several reasons why otherwise talented executives fail to reach their leadership potential. We'll address these and other key issues in the next chapter.

The Essential Elements of Leadership: An Ownership Mind-Set

Can you figure out what you believe, as if you were an owner? Can you find a way to act on those beliefs—alone, or in conjunction with other people? Do you do this with a focus on adding value to others and also take responsibility for the potential negative impact of your actions on others? If you are in charge of others, do you create an environment where your people are empowered, encouraged, and rewarded for acting in this way?

Suggested Follow-Up Steps

- *When were you at your best? What were you doing? What was your mind-set? What environmental factors empowered you to think and act in a way that helped you shine? How does this chapter's definition of leadership shed light on your capacity to be at your best?*

- *What enhances your ability to think and act as if you were an owner? What holds you back from thinking and acting like an owner? What downside risks do you often fear when you think about taking action? What steps could you take to manage your fears and enhance your ability to behave with an ownership mind-set?*

- *Think of a previous leadership situation in which you now, in hindsight, regret your actions. How does this chapter's definition of leadership help explain your regrets? Why did you underperform? What can you learn from this experience?*

- *Are you skeptical about the assertion that you can be a leader today, right now? If so, why? What surprised you as you read this chapter? How might these concepts affect your thinking and change your behavior in your current job or in your community?*

- *If you are in a management position, do you work to create an environment in which your people think and act like owners? What steps could you take that would help you to encourage and be a role model for this behavior? See chapters 3, 4, and 5 for in-depth discussion of this subject.*

- *What's your biggest question—now—regarding leadership?*

CHAPTER TWO

Tackling the Challenges of Leadership

Making a Commitment to Learning, Asking the Right Questions, Seeking Advice, and Fighting Through Isolation

If the essential elements of leadership described in chapter 1 sound pretty straightforward, then why do so many people fail to reach their potential and become leaders? Why is it so darn hard? Why don't more people act like owners?

I used to think that people failed to lead primarily because of a lack of smarts, talent, skills, or experience. In the past several years, though, I have changed my thinking on this question. I have come to believe that, for the most part, people fail to reach their potential and lead because they neglect (or are unable) to build their capacities to clearly understand their situations and, even more importantly, to understand themselves. This can be traced back to their inability to allow themselves to be vulnerable enough to work through the various types of transitions and challenges that they will inevitably face.

Why do people fail to develop or develop and then maintain an ownership mind-set? Why aren't they able to put themselves in the shoes of the decision maker, decide what they believe, determine how to take action, and assess the impact of those actions on others? I believe that this leadership failure tends to result from an inability to address the following interrelated questions:

- Are you confident enough to ask questions and seek advice?

- Are you open to learning or do you think you're supposed to have all the answers?

- Are you emotionally able to withstand feeling vulnerable and comfortable enough to ask for help, admit what you don't know, empower others, and harness the power of your team? Are you comfortable being authentic?

- Do you operate in a manner that causes you to become increasingly isolated?

Thinking and acting as if you are an owner requires hard work. In a complex world, you'll be unlikely to be able do this without the help of others. No one person has enough insight, domain expertise, or perspective to be able to factor in a multitude of considerations and assess the needs of multiple constituencies in any given situation. As a result, a leader needs to learn how to get to conviction on key matters. How can you do this? By developing the ability to ask questions, seek advice, and generally accept that you don't need to have all the answers.

A leader who learns to cultivate others and be open to learning can more effectively fight through the natural isolation that leaders feel as they become more senior. These abilities are essential to thinking and acting as an owner.

In this chapter, we will discuss these questions and explore the reasons why people struggle to reach their potential as leaders. I'll also suggest specific actions you can take to help improve your ability to address these issues and thereby overcome your own unique obstacles to being a more effective leader.

Doing the Work versus a Triumphant Arrival

Leadership takes work. It involves continually being open to learning. It is a process and a journey, much more than it is a destination. You need to accept that there isn't going to be a triumphant arrival. You won't wake up one day and say, "Thank goodness I've finally made it; now I can stop putting all that blood, sweat, and agony into becoming a leader!" Many people feel this way right after they've been promoted to a big job. About a nanosecond later, they begin to realize that they feel even more pressure to prove themselves than they did before the promotion.

What do they do then? Ideally, they realize they have to work just as hard, maybe even harder, to continue to develop their capabilities. How they go about this will determine whether they will grow from that point forward. To many people, this whole cycle of striving, achieving, then feeling more pressure to strive further sounds exhausting. It feels something like being on a treadmill. They don't want to believe that the process of developing into a leader goes on for their entire lives. That just feels too daunting.

If you make the mistake of viewing leadership as a destination—as a state of being—sooner or later you will wind up thinking that you are past the point of needing to work at it. You'll be prone to think that you don't have to keep taking actions that will improve your abilities. Once you believe that you're done learning to be a leader, it becomes a self-fulfilling prophecy: you *are* done developing. In fact, building your capacity to learn and adapt should never end; it should be a lifelong discipline.

This mind-set is an essential element of taking the actions you will need in order to continue your growth and development. The most likely person to derail your progress is not someone else; it's you!

If you are receptive to this way of thinking, let's discuss some simple (maybe even brutally simple) issues for you to address.

Can You Ask a Question?
Can You Seek Advice?

The answer to this one may seem obvious: of *course* you know how to ask a question. We do it all the time. What's the big deal with this?

In fact, it turns out to be a lot more challenging and complicated than most people think. Many otherwise outstanding people reach a point in their lives where they think they are supposed to have all the answers—they think they're supposed to *know*. They're afraid that if they don't act as if they know, they'll appear dumb, or weak, or incapable. If they do ask questions, they may only go through the motions. In other words, they don't actually listen with an open mind and a motivation to learn. Why? They may think it's a sign of weakness to change their minds or be unduly swayed by others. They think that they're now a leader, and a leader (they think) is supposed to have the answers.

Are you open to changing your mind? Can you admit that you were wrong? Do you actively listen and reassess your thinking in response to new facts or persuasive arguments? Your knee-jerk answer may be "of course," but is that really true? How you address these questions has a lot to do with your mental model of leadership, as well as your own emotional makeup. Maybe you believe that leaders are supposed to know what they think and should tell people what to do. Maybe you believe that changing your mind is a sign of weakness, and you need to be resolute. Maybe you have a hard time admitting that you messed up or that you were just plain wrong. If so, you are likely to underperform to your potential.

Are You Listening?

William was the founder and CEO of his own company. While attending the Owner/President Management program at Harvard Business School, he came to see me. He explained that he was concerned that he "wasn't a good leader." Years earlier, he had started his company with a software application that was enormously useful to the firm's customers, most of whom were industrial product manufacturers. Along with a partner, he had developed and then launched the product. After several years, company sales exceeded $25 million, and pretax margins averaged 20 percent. William owned the majority of the equity in the company, and the future was looking bright.

"Sounds great," I said in response to this summary. "So what's the issue?"

"I honestly thought that we had arrived," he responded, "but now I am starting to get worried that our market position is eroding. We are starting to lose business to our archrival competitors. My senior executives follow orders, but they don't seem to care the same way that I do about the future of the company. We need to either be more innovative or market the product better. I really don't know what the issue is. It worries me that we are dealing with these types of issues at this point in our development. Can you help me figure out what's wrong?"

I asked, "What do your senior leaders think?"

He said, "They don't seem to know. They want to know what *I* think, and then want me to tell them what I expect them to do. I am killing myself seeing customers, studying competitors, and thinking about our product. I can't work any harder! I am starting to think that either I have the wrong team or I am managing my team in the wrong way."

He asked if I would talk to his partner, Jim, who was attending the same program. The meeting was set up, and—when the time came—Jim arrived at my office. He didn't hesitate in unloading his frustrations. "William thinks he knows everything," Jim said, with annoyance. "He asks questions, but then interrupts and never allows people to finish. He jumps down our throats, to the point that everyone just wants to figure out what William wants and then figure out how to do it. People have shut down and are afraid to speak up. When they do, he interrogates them and makes them feel stupid." Jim explained that he had articulated his observations to William and encouraged me to raise these issues with him.

At our next meeting, I asked William about Jim's criticisms. He explained to me that this was *his* company, primarily, and that he never stopped feeling the weight of the world on his shoulders. "I'd rather fail doing what *I* believe than fail following someone else's plan," he explained. "No one cares about this company as much as I do. Maybe

I don't trust people as much as I should. But my view of leadership is that I need to *lead*—and that means being strong and pointing the way. Sure, I need to ask questions, but ultimately everyone is looking to me to tell them what to do. I've always run the company this way—and it has worked! Why should I change now?"

I encouraged William to step back and reassess his leadership style. Just because it used to work, I said, doesn't mean it works now. I suggested he take his leadership team off-site when he returned home. "I want you to talk to Jim and agree on a framing of the three or four big issues that face the company," I said. "In the meeting with your team, I want you to lay out each of these questions with the group and then listen to the debate. Your job is to shut up and actively listen. Do not interrupt. Use someone else as the facilitator if you need to. Again: your task should be to frame the questions and then *listen*—no declarative statements!"

William expressed concern that this approach might "freak people out," as he put it. "They are accustomed to me leading!"

I explained to him that my suggested approach *was* "leading." I further explained that there was a time to inquire and a time to advocate, and he needed to learn the difference so that he could train his people to weigh in. After all, they knew as much as he did—and in some cases, probably more—about the intricacies of the business. Moreover, he had to accept that he was unlikely to solve this problem all by himself. He had to find a way to mobilize his team.

William agreed to hold the off-site session. Afterward, he reported that he was amazed how well the meeting had gone: "We came up with a great diagnosis and then three or four concrete actions to address the situation. My people really rose to the occasion. I have to say, I'm shocked at how well this worked."

Separately, Jim told me how pleased he was with the meeting. "So what kind of spell did you put on William?" he asked jokingly. "This was the most effective I've ever seen him as a leader!"

Of course, there was no "spell"; William had simply decided to make a dramatic change in his leadership style. This change, ironically, took a lot of pressure off him and put more on his team. William had to overcome his own concept of leadership, which presumed that asking a question and listening wasn't exercising leadership. He had to learn that one of the roles of a leader is to ask the right questions and then empower his group to step up, debate, and resolve issues.

There is an enormous power asymmetry between the boss and his or her subordinates. The boss has to set the tone for interactions with his team with this imbalance in mind. As a leader, William had to create an environment in which his team members felt empowered to act like owners. To accomplish this, he had to learn to ask a question and then *listen*. Like many entrepreneurs, William needed to learn to adjust his leadership style. For many leaders, there comes a stage in their career when they have to make the shift from "doing everything themselves" to empowering others and working through others to achieve greater success.

If you are not good at asking questions and listening, you are probably not learning as much as you may think. Worse, you may be sending out a vibe that you don't *want* to learn. When this happens, your ability to assess situations and adapt your behavior can quickly erode.

Staying Open to Learning

In many ways, openness to learning is a stages-of-life challenge. When we are students or just starting out in our careers, we are in the mode of asking questions and being open to learning. We are emotionally attuned to playing the student—that is, being a sponge for knowledge. We're not expected to be experts yet. We may not be proactive in getting feedback, but we're usually willing to ask questions and seek advice. This is a mode that comes naturally with getting started in one's life and career.

Of course, even at this stage of life, there are always some people who are guarded and hesitant to reach out. For the most part, though, I have found that young people are normally at their natural peak in terms of proactively seeking to learn. Because they are young, they don't feel awkward about asking a "dumb" question, admitting that they don't know something, and endeavoring to learn. Being a student—or having just recently been a student— makes all of this much easier.

Eventually, a person moves from being a promising young professional to being more advanced in whatever he or she is doing. At some point in a person's life and career, his or her openness to learning can begin to erode, even though he or she is not conscious of this change at all. If you don't make a conscious effort to actively stay in the learning mode, you slowly begin to get out of the habit. Why? As I explained earlier, you get promoted to a job in which you have subordinates and you start to think that, by now, you're supposed to have answers. You become afraid of making yourself look stupid by asking a question that you're probably supposed to know how to answer. Also, the stakes have probably gotten higher, at least in your own mind. In other words, how you appear to others begins to matter more to you.

By this time in your career, you are probably taking on more senior leadership roles, perhaps even joining the board of directors of a for-profit or nonprofit organization. As you do this, unless you improve your abilities to ask questions and learn more proactively, you can find yourself becoming more detached and out of the loop. Typically, you may not even be aware that you are not learning, and instead, you are just trying to fit in.

Her First Nonprofit Board

Jill, an advertising executive, decided to join her first non-profit board of directors. The nonprofit had the mission of helping improve children's literacy and did this by hiring teachers to tutor children after school. Jill had a reasonably good understanding of the program because she had been a volunteer at one of the schools where the program operated. She had been impressed with the positive impact of the program on the children she observed.

Jill attended board meetings for a year. The board met quarterly and included twelve other people, all of whom were successful professionals. The meetings normally consisted of a CEO report, a staff presentation on a specific topic, and a financial discussion that focused on the revenues, expenses, and fund-raising initiatives of the organization.

When she came to see me to catch up, I asked her how she was doing as a relatively new nonprofit board member. "Well," she said, "I think it's going really well. Of course, I like the organization. I like the other board members. I believe in the mission and feel good about spending my time on this."

I asked her about the strengths and weaknesses of the organization, what she thought of the CEO, and how much debate and discussion there was in the board meetings. She hesitated and looked uncomfortable. "What's the matter?" I asked.

She said that she wasn't exactly sure how to answer these questions. She wasn't prepared to comment on the organization's weaknesses. On the positive side, she thought the CEO was solid: "Very articulate with the board, and really cares." Then she volunteered that the board was more in "listening mode" than questioning-and-debating mode.

"Why?" I asked.

She responded, "Well, the board meetings are pretty tightly managed by the chairman, in partnership with the CEO. They seem to have a pretty clear idea of how they want the meeting to go. The chairman feels strongly that the board needs to show its support for the CEO and the staff, so we are always very positive about the reports we hear and there just isn't a lot of pushback. As a new board member, I want to get to know everyone and try to fit in." She paused and added, "It's a great group."

I responded somewhat bluntly. "Sounds to me, Jill, like you don't know much about this organization, and you're so worried about fitting in that you're afraid to ask questions and admit what you don't know. You sound intimidated by the board chairman and maybe even the CEO. Would you let yourself be this clueless and be afraid to ask probing questions at your advertising firm?"

"Well, no—of course not! But that's my day job, and my career is on the line there. My job as a board member is to help raise money and be supportive."

I encouraged her to rethink her approach. Boards of nonprofits need to exhibit leadership, too. The purpose of the board is not to serve as a lapdog to the CEO and chairman. The board has a fiduciary responsibility to understand what's going on and act like owners, even if that approach can be annoying to the organization's managers.

Jill thought about this and decided to try a little different approach. First, she wrote down several key questions she had about the organization. Then she called the CEO and asked for a meeting to go through these questions. At that meeting, she learned a great deal of new information about the organization, and her new understanding prompted some additional questions.

Far from being irritated—as Jill subsequently reported to me—the CEO appeared to be genuinely grateful for

Jill's effort. "Thank you so much for taking such an interest in what we're doing," she said. "Honestly, most of our board members haven't done that, and I'm not sure they understand the range of challenges we're facing. In particular, I am very concerned about recent turnover among the staff, our ability to fund future growth, and whether we need to consider an expanded use of technology with the kids we help. We discuss it among the staff, but I feel like the board doesn't want to hear it. They never ask the obvious questions. Maybe you could help me raise some of these issues at future board meetings?"

Needless to say, Jill was both surprised and pleased. She and the CEO agreed they would speak to the chairman about getting some of these issues on the agenda for the next meeting. The chairman, in turn, was very receptive. It turned out that he had been swamped with his own job and—under time pressure—had reverted to being a process manager at the board meetings. The next board meeting focused on a serious discussion of these key issues. The board loved it, expressing strong opinions and posing a number of follow-up questions. Jill concluded that each of the board members had been assuming that their fellow directors knew what was going on and they hadn't wanted to make waves, look stupid, or disrupt the meetings. They were all relieved when someone on the board took the lead in asking questions they were afraid to ask themselves.

Through this process, Jill learned that raising questions was part of her job as a board member. She also learned that if she was puzzled or worried about something, she probably wasn't alone. Finally, she realized that she could do a lot more to help this organization than she had previously believed. Within two years, she was elected board chairman—one of her proudest career achievements. She felt she was finally really making an impact on the world. How did she accomplish all this? By learning to ask questions and admit what she didn't know.

Can you ask a question? Are you open to learning? It may require exercising a few muscles that you have let atrophy. In particular, it will likely involve dramatically improving your listening skills. Most of all, it may require you to rethink your concept of leadership.

Asking questions and listening are the best ways to stay open to learning. Otherwise, you may put yourself in a situation where everyone around you knows what's going on—everyone, that is, except *you*.

The Creeping Threat of Isolation

Most people readily agree that it is important to avoid isolation. Even if they're not sure exactly what "isolation" is, they know it doesn't *sound* like a good thing.

I define isolation as a situation in which you are unable to see yourself or your circumstances clearly. As a result, your ability to analyze a situation, act, and add value to others is impaired or even undermined.

Of course, we all have our unique blind spots. The question is whether you take steps to identify and understand them. If you don't, you risk developing a *pattern* of blind spots and sustained isolation. Maybe you've observed someone who seems oblivious to a problem he's inadvertently creating for himself and would benefit enormously from getting clued in to his blind spot. *Communication*—being able to ask for feedback as well as receive feedback—is essential to avoiding this type of isolation.

When I speak to executives, they universally agree that isolation is a circumstance to be avoided, and they express sympathy for anyone in this situation. Then, as I discuss with them their own practices, some of them start to turn a little pale as they realize that *they* are in fact much more isolated than they initially realized.

If you fail to ask questions, or if you believe that you're supposed to have all the answers, you are almost certainly sending out a vibe that you don't want to hear what others have to tell you. If you send out this vibe, people around you will gladly oblige you. Life is too short for them to try and puncture your bubble. If you're the boss, moreover, the power asymmetry between you and your subordinates means that your employees don't want to risk upsetting you and certainly will be reluctant to tell you things you need to hear but clearly don't want to hear. Again, you have the power—and therefore the responsibility—to take the first step in seeking comments from others and breaking out of your bubble of isolation.

You may be quite unaware that you're becoming more isolated because this situation usually unfolds gradually over a period of time. To figure out whether you are isolated, ask yourself a series of questions. Do you seek advice? Do you interview your people?

Do you listen without interrupting? Do you usually have a mobile communication device on the table when you are meeting with someone? Are most of your interactions by e-mail, phone, or in person? What practices or early-warning indicators do you have in place to warn you if you have a severe blind spot—for example, an anonymous suggestion box (physical or digital), regular one-on-one meetings with subordinates in which you seek advice, and so on?

A Thoroughbred Racehorse:
The Story of a Superstar

Mario was the brash and charismatic CEO of the Hong Kong subsidiary of a global spirits company headquartered in London. He had been in his current position for about two years. For years, people had told him that he was a "natural leader"—charming, inspirational, and a brilliant strategist. Mario believed that the CEO of his company thought of him as a rising star and a potential leader of the entire company. He had been sent to Hong Kong to get greater executive experience. This rotation was going to last approximately five years, after which he was likely to return to a bigger job at headquarters.

Mario was referred to me through mutual friends who knew I had spent time running businesses in Asia earlier in my career. Mario told me candidly that his experience in Hong Kong had been "difficult" so far. "I am fluent in Mandarin," he said, "which I think is helpful. But I feel that people in the subsidiary look at me with some suspicion. Business results have been stagnant, even though this is supposed to be a growth market for our company. Also, I am not at all happy with some of my key managers, and I have even had to warn one manager that, if he doesn't improve, he will be fired."

He then explained further: "Headquarters has been surprisingly tough to deal with. When I give them a recommendation or make a request, they have sometimes pushed back and rejected my proposals. Sometimes I think the folks back home are a bunch of bureaucrats who'll never understand what it's like to lead in Asia, which is so much harder.

"I am accustomed to getting top-quartile year-end reviews," he continued, "at least until this last year, when I was told that my performance review put me in the second quartile versus my peers. At that session, my direct boss told me there had been several rumblings about my management style. I guess I need to be more touchy-feely or something like that. Anyhow, like I said, this whole situation has been difficult."

I sympathized with Mario. I knew that Asia was, indeed, a very challenging assignment. I warned him that, in my experience, it would be easy to feel like an outsider unless he took conscious and effective steps to fight through isolation. I asked him how he stayed abreast of the business, customers, and his employees: "Who are your key lieutenants? Who do you rely on to answer questions, feed you information, and advise you as to what you should and shouldn't be doing? Also, do you make the rounds among the next level down in order to ask questions and generally get a feel for what's going on in the business?"

"I don't really have that type of setup," Mario responded. "I have a leadership group I meet with every week. We review reports on the business—things like revenues, expenses, and other key metrics—and discuss key initiatives."

I asked again about his confidants—those people of whom he could ask questions and from whom he could seek candid advice, one-on-one. "I really have never had to do that in my previous roles," he said. "I mean, I *do* ask questions, but I'm not that big a fan of all that organizational behavior stuff that other people do. I'm about competence and performance. Set ambitious goals and work to achieve them. In my experience, if you focus on the key elements of the business and demand a high level of quality, your people will rise to the occasion and the business will do well."

I inquired further: "Tell me more about your year-end review. What were the criticisms of you? You mentioned you had fallen into the second quartile. How did your boss explain that?"

Mario elaborated on his previous comment, explaining that criticisms of him came from his subordinates and included descriptors such as *dictatorial*; *doesn't listen*; *doesn't know what he doesn't know*; *is somewhat dismissive of local culture and practices*; *thinks he knows more than he does*.

I was concerned that Mario wasn't more alarmed by this feedback. His year-end review should have been a wake-up call, but he was so concerned with doing things his way that he missed the clear messages that his boss and his people were trying to send to him. So I asked him why he wasn't taking the review more seriously to heart.

He replied, "Listen, I was sent to Hong Kong to fix things. It is natural that I'm going to make some enemies and have people not like me. I've had to shake things up, and negative feedback is par for the course."

Mario's situation reminded me of a case we regularly teach at Harvard Business School, in which a rising star runs into trouble because he fails to learn to adapt his style as he becomes more senior.[1] In addition, I had experienced this type of situation in my own career, so I wanted to give Mario my honest feedback. "Mario," I said, "I think you've missed the forest for the trees. Your job as an expatriate leader is to learn about the business and culture, and to teach and develop the local staff so they can someday take over. Your job is not to be a dictator or star of the show; it is to develop a strong team who can help you run the business. My fear is that you have painted yourself into a corner where everyone around you knows there is a problem—everyone, that is, but you!"

At this point, Mario was beginning to look like he was a bit sorry he had ever come to see me. He said, "Listen, Rob, I know you've had a lot of executive experience, but I don't think you understand what I've had to deal with in turning around this business. You have to break some eggs to make a soufflé."

I laughingly told Mario that I didn't know how to make a soufflé, but that I *did* know how to speak up when I see an issue, even if it wasn't what he wanted to hear. "OK," he said, relaxing a bit. "What, exactly, are you suggesting I do?"

"First and foremost, I'd like you to consider making some changes to your style. Everything I'm going to suggest is intended to help make you less isolated, so that you can understand your situation far more clearly. First, pick your top three to five lieutenants. Meet with each one-on-one and ask them for one or two suggestions about what you could do better or do differently in order to improve your performance. Listen hard to what they say and even take notes. If they seem afraid to give you a suggestion, be patient and urge them to give you advice.

"Maybe that's enough for a start. My fear is that you are doing way too much directing and not nearly enough inquiry and listening. As a result, I think you are not getting the best from your people, and are failing to understand yourself and your situation clearly."

Even though he was somewhat skeptical, he decided to give this exercise a try. A short time later, I heard from him. He was shocked by the response of his people, he told me. His subordinates had been waiting for an opportunity to tell him what they thought—about the business and, to some extent, about his approach. They believed the business had the wrong people in the wrong seats. They believed the marketing strategy was out of date and more suited to Europe than to Hong Kong. They explained that Mario's fluency in the local language did not equate with understanding the local culture and consumer tastes. They urged him to reverse some of his previous decisions and change the way he made decisions—starting with involving *them* in the decision-making process.

Mario told me that, after his initial shock, he continued to be unsettled by this experience, mainly because he realized they were right. It didn't necessarily feel good, but he had to agree with them. All of a sudden, he began to better understand why some of his key decisions seemed to have flopped. He realized that working *with* this team was going to yield far superior results to going it alone, in a top-down fashion.

I enjoyed watching this story unfold. Mario was the thoroughbred racehorse who until recently had gone unbeaten in every outing. He had the magic touch and could do no wrong—that is, until he got more senior in his career and was put in a situation where he needed help. It had only been a matter of time. The good news was that he learned valuable lessons before it was too late.

I've said that isolation emerges as a greater danger as you get older and become more senior. However, younger people aren't immune to isolation. You need to start thinking about isolation—and how to avoid it—early in your career and life.

The Millennials

The millennial generation is the most connected, best networked, and—theoretically—best informed in history. After all, technology is at their fingertips, and they are expert at using it. In theory, we should thank our lucky stars that we finally have a generation that has figured out how to interact, build relationships, and avoid isolation.

It would be great if that were true. In fact, I have been surprised at how often the *opposite* is true.

In my role at Harvard, I've had the opportunity to have conversations with a multitude of men and women in their mid- to late twenties. Our initial discussions tend to be about school, career choices, and the like. After several months, when a student comes back for a second or third conversation, the topics start to change. In many cases, students eventually broach a serious subject—one that they are hesitant to discuss because it is deeply personal and maybe a little embarrassing. For example, it might have to do with deep self-doubt, relationships with a parent or loved one, or fear regarding the future.

In such cases, the first question I tend to ask is whether they have discussed this issue with someone else. Most frequently, their answer is, "No, not with anyone." Sometimes I repeat their answer back to them to make sure I've understood them correctly. "Yes, that's right," they respond. "You heard me correctly. I haven't talked to anyone until now."

I ask, *"Why?* Surely there must be someone in your life with whom you can discuss this kind of issue?" Again, their answer is almost always in the negative: "No, no one."

After having engaged in many of these conversations, I began to realize that the millennial generation is, on balance, far more isolated than mine. But how can that be? They all have numerous social-media networks. They text, tweet, and follow each other's activities on Facebook, Instagram, and so on. They are avid users of e-mail.

But here's the issue: because they have all these communication options, they too often substitute indirect contact for face-to-face conversations. They text when they should phone; they phone when they should meet in person; they use remote forms of communication that don't foster the development of relationships.

At the same time, there is an inherent lack of privacy in many of these modes. Whatever gets posted on a particular site may spread virally to unintended recipients. To deal with this challenge, people can get in the habit of wearing a mask with their peers. This poses a potential problem: the habit can become so ingrained that they begin to also wear an attractive disguise even in their closest relationships.

As a result, they spend less time having candid face-to-face communications and become less practiced at disclosing real issues they are facing. If they can't reveal their most challenging problems and insecurities to a close friend or loved one, they will almost certainly struggle to get helpful advice regarding how to deal with these issues. This isolation may cause them to think less clearly and make decisions that they ultimately regret.

The Fear of Feeling Vulnerable by Being Yourself

Asking questions, admitting you need to learn, and breaking through isolation all take practice and also require a degree of self-confidence. Ironically, many people think this type of behavior reflects a *lack* of confidence. As discussed earlier, most of us hate the thought of looking weak or stupid. Most of us hate doing things that make us feel less powerful. If you haven't practiced this—or if you have a history of unpleasant experiences in these situations—you may simply not be able to stand putting yourself in this position.

You may feel vulnerable and not know why. It may have something to do with your life story—for example, with a past experience of trusting someone and subsequently feeling betrayed. You may have strained relationships with one or more parents or other experiences that have conditioned you to avoid situations in which you feel dependent on others.

The problem is that leadership *must* involve working with others and accepting some degree of dependence on others.

For some people, the hesitancy to be authentic stems from their secretly held view of themselves. Maybe they believe they are imposters, or really are stupid, or aren't good enough to be in their current job, or lack other key attributes that simply make them inferior to those around them. This may help explain why they are hesitant to speak up, confront a colleague when there's a real issue, give feedback to a subordinate, or share their concerns with their colleagues so they can work together to address them. We'll talk much more in the next chapter about the critical importance of getting better at understanding yourself as you move through transitions in your life.

Transitions Expose Problems

Normally, people don't become fully aware of their degree of isolation until they experience a transition. A transition could be a promotion, a new job, a new geographic location, a change in your personal or family life, or a change in your team. It could be triggered by retirement. Transitions can also be triggered by changes in the economy, your industry, the life cycle of a key product, or actions by competitors.

Whatever the catalyst, transitions create a heightened burden on leaders to accurately assess their situation and adapt to it appropriately. It means the context is changing, and you eventually will find yourself out of alignment if you fail to adapt. These adaptive behaviors may involve changing strategy, your people, or your leadership style.

If you are isolated, you are far less likely to see the situation clearly or make changes to your own leadership approach on a timely basis. Too often, executives fail because they don't recognize transitions soon enough to prevent a terrible problem or capitalize on a huge opportunity. Postmortems on leadership failures are full of stories about people with deep regrets regarding their failure to recognize a transitional challenge soon enough to address it.

Practice Makes Perfect— or at Least, Better

I hope this chapter has inspired you to revisit your notion of the nature of leadership.

Developing as a leader is an ongoing process. Like most processes, it requires hard work and persistence. Asking questions, being open to learning, fighting through isolation, and recognizing transitions are all challenging tasks. They require you to tolerate some degree of vulnerability.

In my experience, the more you work at it, the more adept you will become.

The next chapter delves much more deeply into the steps and processes that you need to master in order to become a better leader. Following these steps should help you to dramatically improve your ability to figure out what you believe and act in a way that adds value to others.

Suggested Follow-Up Steps

- *Describe your leadership style. How does your leadership style enhance your effectiveness? How does your style undermine your leadership effectiveness?*

- *In particular, do you ask questions, seek advice, ask for feedback, and delegate to others? Are you open to saying "I don't know," "I've changed my mind," "I would like your advice," "I was wrong . . ."? If you're unable to do these things, why?*

- *How do you go about making an important decision? As a result of reading this chapter, how might you change your decision processes?*

- *What creates stress and vulnerability for you? What is your failure narrative (see chapter 3)? How are these factors undermining your ability to be an effective leader?*

- *What actions do you take to push back or punch through isolation?*

CHAPTER THREE

Mastering the Essential Processes of Leadership

A Regimen for Learning How to Think and Act Like an Owner

In chapter 1, we discussed the key elements of leadership and the importance of establishing an ownership mind-set. In chapter 2, we talked about the issues that prevent leaders from taking ownership and the essential need to be continually open to learning in order to overcome isolation. If this framing resonates with you, it is now time to take steps to improve your leadership abilities and address likely pitfalls that could cause you to fall short.

Leadership is very much about learning. To facilitate this learning, there are processes you will need to master that will help you develop your capacities to lead and enhance your ability to think and act like an owner.

It's a Process versus a Destination

There are at least two leadership-related processes that we go through every day. We may not be explicitly *aware* that we are engaging in these processes, but they are taking place nevertheless. The issue is whether we are consciously engaging in them in a disciplined and proactive way—striving to do them well—or dealing with them in a haphazard way, which is likely to undermine our development and our performance.

The first process I'll refer to as "vision, priorities, and alignment." This is a strategic process that deals primarily with identifying and articulating how you distinctively add value, prioritizing critical tasks essential to adding that value, and making sure that your management decisions are aligned with accomplishing these aspirations. For a more in-depth discussion of this process, you can refer to my book *What to Ask the Person in the Mirror.*[1]

The premise of this approach is that leadership is about framing the right questions rather than having all the answers. Effective leaders must make sure their organizations are focused on adding value that is distinctive and making decisions that are aligned with achieving their aspirations.

There is also a second process silently taking place alongside the first. It is less intellectual—and in some ways scarier—than the first because it is about *you*. This process is about understanding yourself and developing habits that will enable you to keep learning about yourself. For a more in-depth discussion of this second process, you can refer to my book *What You're Really Meant to Do*.[2]

The central premise of this approach is that understanding yourself is critical to your ability to learn to become an effective leader. While that may sound painfully obvious, the truth is that many people don't work at understanding themselves and fail to connect this understanding to learning to think and act as an owner.

At various points in their lives and careers, many talented people encounter challenging situations—usually transitions—in which they can analyze the situation, but they're unable to figure out why they are doing what they are doing. As a result, they fail to reach their leadership potential. The process of understanding is intended to help you address these challenges by laying out a lifelong regimen of steps to improve your self-awareness and channel this understanding into improving your leadership development.

Maybe you read the previous two paragraphs and are saying something to the effect of, "I have absolutely no idea what he's talking about. I am definitely not aware of or involved in *either* of those processes." My response would be to reiterate that, although you may not be consciously aware of them or actively engaged in them, these processes *are* taking place nevertheless.

In particular, articulating a clear vision, setting priorities, and creating alignment is a regimen you ought to be consciously engaged in on a daily basis. Similarly, your ability to understand yourself comes into play every single day, in every action that you take or don't take. Think of these processes as streams of activities that are happening right in front of you. The question is whether you open your eyes to these streams and proactively manage them, rather than doing whatever comes up and wondering what happened when things go wrong.

To reiterate, leadership is about learning and continuing to learn. Thinking and acting like an owner involves learning to explore intellectual as well as emotional matters. It involves knowing what to pay attention to in the chaos of your work and life, and knowing how to better understand yourself. This chapter will delve into these processes and talk about why they are central to you becoming a leader, improving as a leader, and avoiding being derailed as a leader. Once again, if leadership involves asking the right questions and being open to learning, these two processes are primary streams on which to focus this effort.

Vision, Priorities, and Alignment

Articulating a clear vision, identifying three to five top priorities, and then assessing whether you are in or out of alignment: these are steps you can take to dramatically improve your leadership effectiveness. It is analogous to taking a trip in your car. Where are we going? Why are we going there? What are the most important things we need to do to get there? Once we start the trip, are we on course or off course? These are key questions to ask when you are taking a trip, and they're just as critical when taking your leadership journey. They are also critical to empowering those around you to think and act as owners. If your team has a shared understanding of where you're going, it's much easier for them to proactively take actions that will help the organization to get there.

Vision

A vision is an aspiration. It is the articulation of how an enterprise adds value to others in a way that is *distinctive*. As discussed in earlier chapters, an essential element of leadership is a focus on adding value to others. By "adding value," I mean the benefit the organization creates for its customers or other key constituencies it is trying to serve. The emphasis on the word "distinctive" indicates that the organization must create a product or service that adds value that is above and beyond other relevant alternatives. It must be better than, or a critical complement to, other comparable offerings for some segment of the market. Put another way, what benefit would the world lose if this particular company or nonprofit organization did not exist?

This element is vital to inspiring people to get out of bed in the morning and be excited about contributing to the cause. I have yet to encounter a leader or an organization that has had success over a sustained period of time without focusing intensely on continually asking and answering this question. To be sure, I've seen certain leaders and businesses enjoy success over a relatively brief period, but if they did not focus on how to add distinctive value to others, their success ultimately did not last.

By this way of thinking, profitability is an outcome that comes as a result of adding value that is distinctive. This is why most excellent business leaders and organizations own the responsibility of serving their customers with superb offerings and regularly update their thinking on how to improve those offerings. Making money will occur as a result of relentless accomplishment of this objective. I have regularly seen businesses get themselves in trouble, and ultimately begin to lose money or even fail, because their leadership began to focus first on making money. They made the mistake of beginning to believe that profit itself was the vision, rather than adding value to their customers.

So leaders need to ask and re-ask this question: how do we add value that is distinctive? They must take ownership of this challenge. It is the prism through which they judge everything they do. To accomplish this, they have to go one step further, regularly articulating that vision to their employees and other key constituencies. Additionally, they have to make sure that their employees do the same with *their* direct reports and key constituencies.

In this way, they improve the ability of their employees to think and act as owners. It empowers employees to figure out what they believe and then act on those beliefs. When the vision is clear, the organization's employees are much more likely to pull in the same direction because they have a keen and shared focus on how to add value. By the same token, when employees see cracks in the company's ability to add value, they are empowered to raise their hand and flag the problem to senior managers so that they can address the issue and make changes. In this way, employees are serving a cause greater than themselves. They are acting like owners.

This is an ongoing process. Because the world is constantly changing, it is unlikely that the way you created value even a few years ago is still adding as much value today. Why? Product life cycles, product commoditization, globalization, technological innovation, and changes in societal norms and consumer behaviors occur continuously. Sooner or later, these changes alter your value proposition. This is why leaders have to be consistently open to learning in order to regularly update their value proposition. How do we add value that is distinctive? This question must be asked regularly in order for a leader to stay ahead of the curve.

Vision is the "why" of what the company is doing every single day. It is a powerful vehicle, tool, and lens for leaders and their employees.

Priorities

Establishing a clear vision is not enough. A leader has to take this vision and break it down into a manageable number of key priorities, ideally no more than three to five. These priorities are the tasks that the organization needs to execute at a high level of quality in order to add value that is distinctive. I say "three to five" because having ten priorities is the same as having none. Most leaders find that they can't adequately focus their organization on more than a few key priorities if they hope to execute them at a high level of excellence.

Examples of top priorities might be: attract, retain, and develop key staff; build superb relationships with key customers; innovate new products and services; invest in world-class information technology to manage inventory and analyze customer information; and so on.

A leader needs to work with his or her team to figure out what these top priorities ought to be. This typically takes a lot of thought and agonizing. Why? Choosing one priority usually means that you are implicitly not choosing another. This exercise is about making *choices* and weighing *trade-offs*. Explicitly identifying your top priorities will empower your people to exercise their best judgment in those situations where they must make trade-off decisions.

Making choices about your priorities may take weeks of thought and study. For example, you may need to interview your customers to discuss the key drivers of the value they believe you add. These drivers should link directly to your choice of top priorities.

CHOOSING PRIORITIES FOR FASHION APPAREL

I worked as an adviser with a company that designed and produced fashion apparel for women. Its leaders believed that the company's distinctive value was to anticipate the latest women's fashion trends and design merchandise that was in line with these trends. In addition, it provided intensive service to its retail store clients so that they could help customers create an integrated ensemble. By bringing together fashion and service, the company helped its customers look stylish and unique. When a customer wore one of this company's dresses to an event, she knew that she would look fashionable, and that it was highly unlikely that any other woman at the event would be wearing something similar.

The CEO of this company believed that, in order to add this value, the company needed to hire the very best designers in the world, use only the highest-quality materials, and charge a premium price to justify the enormous investment in time and materials. At the same time, the distribution channel had to be consistent with premium quality at a premium price. In keeping with this priority, the CEO said no to various retail chains that proposed to carry its merchandise, because he believed it was inconsistent with the brand and value proposition. The company's vision and these priorities were clearly and repeatedly articulated to every employee, and served as the lens through which they assessed every decision they made.

This company is an excellent example of the need to have a clearly articulated theory regarding three to five top priorities. If you begin to believe that your prioritization is out of date, you need to ask questions and engage your team to figure out how to adjust your priorities. This is no small task. Specific priorities are the drivers of how company employees spend their time. As such, they need to be carefully developed and then communicated regularly to the entire firm.

There is usually a second step in this process. While the entire organization has to have priorities, each business unit also should have its own adapted set of key priorities.

In other words, each department of a company contributes to the vision in its own unique way. For example, the IT department needs to determine its top-three priorities and how it adds value to the organization, so that the company can achieve its overarching vision. The same goes for the legal department, human resources, manufacturing, the Japanese subsidiary, and so on. This exercise becomes a discipline that cascades through the enterprise.

The key challenge for you as a leader is whether you are sufficiently focused on establishing and communicating key priorities in your organization. Even if you are not, rest assured that your firm and your units will have *some* set of priorities that they are acting upon. The problem is, these priorities will vary by individual and leader depending on their own interpretation of what the overall enterprise is trying to do. In my experience, this haphazard approach to priority setting creates confusion, results in people working at cross-purposes, and ensures that employees are not certain of what they're supposed to be doing. Obviously, this kind of confusion can undermine the ability of employees to think and act like owners. As a result, they are likely to be less effective and feel less empowered, which will ultimately result in underperformance on the part of both the leader and the organization.

Alignment

Once you've articulated a clear vision with specific priorities, your focus can then turn to the myriad of decisions that you make every day. In particular, you must focus on making sure that your decisions—large and small—are consistent with achieving your vision and executing the associated priorities.

The word "alignment" captures this idea. Alignment is akin to getting the wheels on your car adjusted so that everything is pulling in the same direction. With each action you take, you must explicitly consider whether it helps get you into alignment or risks pushing you out of alignment.

As such, you should be assessing the impact on alignment every time you make a decision. Your people should be trained to take ownership of doing the same. This can happen if you engage your team in a disciplined process of articulating a clear vision, identifying a manageable number of priorities, and assessing each of your key decisions based on its positive (or negative) impact on alignment.

DESIGN FACTORS

The decisions you make every day usually deal with one or more design factors. They include:

- The people you hire. What is the profile of the people you hire? What level of education, technical skills, years of experience, and so on, are required? What are their personal characteristics in terms of age, ambition, work ethic, personality type, diversity, and so on? All of these factors should be considered regularly. Thinking about them explicitly— in particular, whether they help you get further in or out of alignment with achieving your vision and priorities—is critically important.

- Key tasks. What are the key tasks you must do well
  to achieve the vision and priorities? Every business
  or nonprofit has a range of tasks the leaders must
  execute if the enterprise is to succeed. They vary
  by type of business and industry. Can you list the
  four or five that are most critical to your enterprise?
  These tasks are not passed down like the Ten Com-
  mandments from the heavens; they are *decided*—by
  you or someone else. It is important to ask whether
  you have selected and are focused on the right tasks.

- Formal organization. These are design factors relat-
  ing to organizational reporting structure—where
  you locate people physically; how you pay, promote,
  and evaluate your people; types of meetings with
  personnel; and all the myriad processes that go into
  designing and running an organization. You may
  take many of these factors and processes for granted.
  This would be a mistake. Making these choices and
  processes explicit helps you focus on whether they
  are still in alignment with achieving the vision and
  accomplishing the priorities.

- Your leadership style. How do you lead? Can you
  write down a detailed description of your style?
  Are you confrontational, do you like one-on-one or
  group meetings, are you a delegator, are you a coach,
  are you open or guarded, do you actively communicate to make your views clear, what do you do
  when things go wrong, and so on? Your leadership
  style can have a powerful impact on your alignment.

Are you aware of your own style? Start by writing it down.

- Culture. These are the norms—the "should do's" and "shouldn't do's" of your organization. They are typically influenced by industry and company context, the people you hire, the tasks you ask them to perform, the formal organizational elements of the firm (including structure and key incentives), and your leadership style. Cultures are neither good nor bad in and of themselves, but either they can help create alignment with achieving the vision and priorities, or they can undermine achieving alignment. Here, the analysis begins with writing down an accurate description of the culture and then asking the questions about alignment. To change the culture, you will likely need to change one or more of the key design factors. A superb speech, all by itself, won't do the trick unless it is backed up by changes to specific design factors.

Based on your analysis of these design factors, sketch out two columns on a piece of paper: one labeled "in," and one labeled "out." Take a stab at listing the elements of your organization that are in versus out of alignment.

Most organizations are in alignment in some areas and out of alignment in others. Events are regularly occurring that cause you to get out of alignment—a competitor takes a key action, the economy turns down, a key employee quits, you get bored and change your leadership style, and so on. In addition, some of your decisions may inadvertently cause you to get out of alignment, particularly if you don't fully consider the consequences of your decisions on achieving your vision and priorities. This is why you need to ask these questions on some regular basis, and use vision and priorities as a prism for making decisions.

Change management strategies are intended to address those areas that you identify as being out of alignment. The purpose of making changes is to help get you back into better alignment with achieving your vision and accomplishing your key priorities.

THE CLEAN SHEET OF PAPER EXERCISE

If you like this way of analyzing your organization, one exercise you can conduct is a "clean sheet of paper" analysis. This involves assembling a diverse group of four or five of your up-and-coming leaders and asking them to consider the following questions:

- If we were starting the organization from scratch, how would we change the design factors?

- In particular, do we have the right people, are we performing the right tasks, do we have the right pay and promotion processes, and do our leaders have the right leadership style?

- If not, what changes would you make to these design factors?

This can be a fabulous way to get dispassionate advice and provides a great learning experience for your up-and-coming leaders. It gives them a chance to think and act like owners at an earlier stage in their careers. You may not agree with everything they advise, but you will almost certainly get three or four superb ideas that will improve your organization. This is, in effect, a way to address your blind spots by getting some perspective from people who are likely to have a bit of emotional distance because they were probably not the ones who designed your current organization.

SUMMING UP: THE ALIGNMENT CHALLENGE

Who do we hire, who do we fire, where should our people sit, how do we pay people, how do we handle health-care benefits, what type of product distribution makes sense, should we send employees to a industry conference in Las Vegas, should I confront a key employee regarding a mistake or let it go, should I delegate a certain task or do it myself, and so on? These are the kinds of questions you ask every day. Each decision you make should be through the lens of whether this decision helps you achieve the vision and accomplish your key priorities.

Mastering the Process: Vision, Priorities, and Alignment

Vision and priorities, taken together, create a prism through which you should be judging every action you take. Without a clear articulation, you and your employees will too often be unsure as to what to do. Under pressure, people tend to "go with their gut," or do what they think you'd want them to do, or simply do what is expedient. Or they may be unable to decide and therefore do nothing.

As we've discussed, leadership is about deciding what you believe as if you were an owner and acting in a way that adds value to others. If you accept this proposition, then you need to go through a systematic and disciplined process of figuring out how your company, and each of its subunits, adds value. You need to make sure that you and the organization are clear on this vision and then identify a small number of associated key priorities. With these building blocks in place, you can then work to create an aligned organization that you and your employees are empowered to drive.

This process may not sound all that exciting, but believe me, it is the nuts and bolts of leadership. Leadership is ultimately about what you do: your *actions*. Eloquent words are important at times, but leadership ultimately is about what you do. Vision, priorities, and alignment are how you create a game plan to decide what to do and then *succeed* at what you do.

The Second Process Integral to Ownership: Understanding Yourself

There is a second process going on, in parallel with vision, priorities, and alignment. This second process is more amorphous and—for many people—more troubling and even scary. As discussed earlier, many of us are only vaguely aware of it, and many would prefer for it to stay that way. Why? It is about *you*.

When I speak to executives about this subject, they might say something like, "Hey, I thought you were a businessperson, not a touchy-feely psychologist! What does this mumbo jumbo have to do with leadership—or with business, for that matter? I'm trying to make money (or run a nonprofit, or win an election), and I don't have time to get wrapped up in navel gazing or pondering the meaning of life. I've got a job to do and an organization to run!"

I get this point of view, because I used to think this way myself. I started thinking more about this subject when I began to realize that my emotional reactions to certain business situations were undermining my ability to perform, and I didn't fully understand why I was acting the way I was acting. I began to learn (and am still learning) that I couldn't reach my potential if I wasn't willing to look in the mirror and ask some tough questions—about myself.

Understanding yourself is not something you can run away from or set off to the side to deal with some other time. You have to own this process. Your capacity to understand yourself has an impact on your ability to do your job every day. The essential question is whether you are open to being aware and learning about yourself, or whether you are simply unwilling to go there. When I talk to leaders about being open to learning, asking questions, and avoiding isolation, they tend to nod their heads enthusiastically: "Yes, I agree; that's a good thing." But when they realize that I'm telling them that this includes a willingness to ask questions and learn about who they are, their enthusiasm tends to fade. "So this is really a key part of my leadership development?" Yep, it really is.

Do you know *why* you do what you do? Do you understand your tolerance for risk and your trigger points for stress? Think of all the actions you take during a day: juggling tasks large and small, analyzing specific situations, talking to people, (hopefully) asking questions, pretending you know something you don't, confronting people or being afraid to confront people, losing your temper, being afraid to show anger or emotions, consoling your staff, seeking advice, persuading, getting persuaded, and so on. How and why you do all these activities are heavily influenced by who you are.

Do you know why you do what you do? Why can't I delegate? Why do I delegate too much? Why can't I confront people? Why am I too confrontational? Why can't I admit I made a mistake? Why can't I admit I was wrong? Why can't I change my mind? For most of us, the list goes on and on. As a leader, you have to keep updating your understanding of why you do what you do. If you are willfully unaware of this, you are probably much more isolated than you may realize. As described earlier, you are likely to be in a situation where everyone around you knows there's a problem—everyone, that is, but you!

Strengths and Weaknesses

The process of understanding yourself starts with writing down your strengths and weaknesses. This seems as if it should be simple, but for many people, it's an exercise they are unable to do accurately.

Why? First, all of us have blind spots, and as a result, we need to seek and be open to receiving feedback from those who observe us, especially when it comes to being made aware of our weaknesses. Of course, people will only be willing to give you this feedback if you ask for it in a way that suggests you are highly receptive; they don't want to offend you, and they'll need to be certain that you want to hear constructive criticism. No one wants to take the risk of hurting your feelings and having you dislike them as a result. So taking ownership of this process means you have to explicitly seek out help, listen without arguing, and make sure people know you appreciate them sticking their neck out to help you.

This is enormously uncomfortable for many people, particularly if they are insecure or—worse—think they are such big shots that they must not show any weakness by seeking advice or help. Those who refuse to reach out are likely to find that their weaknesses increasingly hinder their effectiveness, until an event happens that does some lasting damage to their careers and their reputations. Often, this is a self-inflicted wound: one that could have been avoided by having the humility and the motivation to ask for feedback regarding weaknesses.

The purpose of this analysis is not to immediately jump to developing an action plan for addressing your weaknesses. The first step is *becoming more aware*. The analysis comes first; developing a strategy for addressing your skills comes second. Certain weaknesses are not worth trying to fix. For example, if you are not analytical, it may be difficult for you to take extensive actions that would help you become a lot more analytical. Also, it may not be necessary to address this weakness, depending on the needs of your job and the composition of your team.

One productive exercise is to decide what tasks need to be accomplished in your current job in order for you to perform at a high level of competence. You then need to figure out how those tasks fit with your strengths and weaknesses. For those key tasks that don't fit your skills, you can assess whether a strategy of delegating those tasks to team members can be effective. A good example of this is the emergence of technology and social media skills necessary in various businesses. Leaders don't need to become immediately expert or even particularly fluent in technology, but they *do* need to make sure that their team includes someone who has this competence.

These judgments start with creating self-awareness and then thinking through tactical options to help you perform your job at a high level. Excellent leaders learn that they don't need to be great at everything, and they don't need to stubbornly try to do everything themselves. They learn to become more self-aware, assemble a team with requisite skills, and get better at delegating.

Strengths and weaknesses are not absolutes. They are always relative to a job or a task. As you change jobs, your relevant strengths and weaknesses will change accordingly. For example, the level of writing skills you may need to be a businessperson are going to be wholly different than you'd need if you decided to become a college professor of English. The skills needed to manage five employees may be very different than if you go to a job where you are managing five hundred people across a wide variety of functions. The point is to calibrate your skills in light of the top three or four tasks you must perform at a high level of competence in your current or prospective job. This means doing a study of a particular job to determine those three or four top tasks. The question you should be regularly asking is: *What skills does it take to be great at my job?*

This process will require you to improve your ability to solicit feedback, think through the needs of a particular job, and figure out the matches and mismatches with your skills.

Understanding your strengths and weaknesses is a key building block of being a leader. If you're trying to figure out what you believe and take action with an ownership mind-set, you will need to understand your skills. Understanding those skills—and limitations—will make it far easier for you to identify where you need help from others in analyzing a situation and determining a plan of action.

Passion

Once you figure out your skills, you need to move to figuring out what you love to do. *Passion is the rocket fuel that drives high performance.* Performing analyses, figuring out how to take action, agonizing over the vision and priorities of the company, and doing all the other things you need to do to be an effective leader are a whole lot easier if you like what you're doing and believe in the organization's mission. No matter how much you like your job, there are going to be bad days, bad weeks, and bad months. A passion for what you're doing is what pulls you through those stretches.

Understanding yourself means understanding what you love to do and what brings out your passions. This will vary by job, stage of life, changes in the world, and a host of other factors. As a result, understanding your passion is a lifelong challenge you have to work at. You have to take ownership of this challenge.

WHAT'S NEXT?

I was meeting with John, a seventy-four-year-old former executive who was trying to figure out what he wanted to do next in his life. He joked with me that he had "flunked retirement." After selling his business, being free from daily responsibility sounded great to him—at first. He enjoyed the first several months of being with his wife and family full-time. He was in good health, and—as time went on—he began to realize that he had many more productive years ahead of him. He also knew that he wanted to be relevant and engaged in the world. He wanted to be useful to society. He didn't want to be a bystander. He came to me looking for advice as to how he might think about his next chapter.

I asked him, "What do you love to do?"

After several minutes of silence, John answered, "I'm kind of embarrassed to admit it, but I don't think I know.

I mean, I liked being a company executive, but I think I stopped thinking about what I enjoyed at work a long time ago."

This wasn't all that unusual and didn't surprise me. I asked him to reflect: "John, think about a time you were at your best. What were you doing? What were the tasks? Why did you like it so much? Why did you shine?"

Ironically, after further thought, he didn't refer back to an experience from his business career. Instead, he talked about a volunteer stint he did over a weekend for Habitat for Humanity. This volunteer assignment had been organized by his company, and he absolutely loved it. Why? He recalled enjoying the comradeship, the act of building something tangible, and knowing that he and his colleagues were helping displaced families. The entire experience made him feel vital and at his best.

I asked him exactly what he did on this project that was so rewarding. He said that he applied his organizational skills and used his leadership experience to help the group work as a cohesive team. He coached people how to learn construction skills, figure out the critical tasks, learn to orchestrate those tasks, and work together cooperatively. He recalled that it seemed to be a great learning experience for everyone—and all with a focus on helping others.

"OK," I responded. "Based on this experience, what insights do you take away that can help you better understand what you might love to do?"

Over the next few weeks, John thought about his situation. He began looking for projects in his community where he might bring to bear his executive skills and coaching experience. He ultimately found two such opportunities in the nonprofit sector. John joined both boards, became chairman of one of them, and in both cases got actively involved in coaching the CEO. Months later, he reported back to me that he was "having a ball!" He had found a way to move to the next stage of his life. This next phase might not have been what John originally expected, but it made him feel alive, relevant, and energized, because it reconnected him with his passions.

Finding your passion is critical at each stage of your life—at the start of your career, through your various career moves, and even after it seems that your professional life is over. Improving your openness to understand your own passions and interests may take you places you didn't expect to go, but those places may turn out to be incredible. I never expected to be a professor at Harvard; it would not have even been on my list of possibilities. However, after working to better understand my passions, I realized that it was a fantastic fit—at least for now.

That's another related and key point: the world is changing. Every one of us is changing. Your passions are going to change accordingly. Pay attention.

The truth is that *you can add value to others throughout your life*. Get in the habit of trying to understand your passions. It will help you to shine. It will also serve as an excellent lens for deciding how to structure your job at work, what to delegate, and how to identify your dream job at every stage of your life.

Your Story

Your leadership style and the actions you take are heavily influenced by your life story—the events in your life that help shape who you are. This is a little more complex than it initially sounds. Most of us have *three* stories: the basic facts, the success story, and a failure narrative.

The basic facts of the story are clear enough; this is literally the chronology of key events in your life. Even if the facts of your life may seem obvious, I recommend that you take the time to write them down. The simple act of writing the chronology is likely to remind you of events from your past—things that your conscious mind may have long since forgotten, but might have somehow stayed with you in the back of your mind. Surfacing them may help you understand some things better or identify patterns of behavior you have failed to recognize.

The success story is the positive spin you put on those basic facts. Most people have so much practice telling the success story that I don't need to prompt them much to tell it; they've gotten so good at it. The success narrative takes the facts of your life and turns them into an inspiring tale of encountering and overcoming obstacles, experiencing setbacks and rebounding after the setbacks, and so on. This narrative may have several twists and turns, but always has the same punch line—you are the hero of the story. Even when you are trying to downplay your successes and speak candidly about setbacks and failures, you are likely to follow up by explaining how these failures turned out to be a positive thing, because they enabled you to grow and reach greater heights.

The problem with the success story is that even though it's the story you tell others, it is all too often *not* the story you tell yourself. In fact, you may not fully believe every aspect of this story, even though you regularly tell it with great gusto. This brings us to the "failure narrative," sometimes referred to as the "self-doubt" narrative.

This story takes the same basic facts of your life and spins them into a tale of uncertainty, insecurity, and self-doubt. Most likely, it's a story you don't have much practice telling, because it's one that you usually keep to yourself. It may be a story of insecurities, negative thoughts about your own character, doubts about your abilities, and forebodings about the consequences of trusting others. Even though you don't tell the story very often—if at all—it is still a story that is rattling around in your head. It may be the story you think of when you lose your temper, decline to speak up, act politically, or fail to figure out what you truly believe. It is usually based on searing events in your life that taught you mixed lessons: for example, difficult relationships with your parents, getting fired, betrayal by someone you trusted, the breakup of a romantic relationship, or getting passed over for promotion.

While I don't care much if you write down your success story, I would like you to write down your failure narrative, even if you don't intend for anyone else to ever see it.

Why go through this potentially painful exercise? The purpose in eliciting this narrative is not to make you feel bad or help you get this story out of your mind; you won't. The purpose of this exercise is to help you become more *aware of it and how it might be having an impact on your behavior.* Is it playing a role in sabotaging your efforts to become a leader?

Do you know?

NOT GOOD ENOUGH

Anne was an outstanding vice president in a large and successful technology company. She had been valedictorian of her high school class in the Midwest and finished at the top of her class in college. She had succeeded at almost everything she had tried in her life. She was a superb high school swimmer, as well as an excellent pianist. Upon graduation from college, she had numerous attractive job offers, including one from her current firm.

One of her college professors asked if I would give her a little advice. He explained that she was deciding whether or not to stay with her current company, and he was concerned about her rationale and decision-making process.

In my office, Anne explained her thinking. "I don't feel that I'm doing very well at my company, and so I'm thinking about looking for another job."

I asked, "Why do you say you're not doing well?"

She responded, "I just feel like I'm not getting great promotion opportunities, and I'm not really sure about my future at the company."

I asked her to give me the full chronology of her five years at the company. She proceeded to tell a story of regular promotions, top quartile reviews, and top quartile compensation. In short, it sounded to me as if she was doing very well and had a very bright future at this firm. So, why did Anne feel this way? She couldn't really explain; it was just her instinct that it wasn't going so well.

I shifted gears and asked Anne to tell me about her life story. She did. I then explained the failure narrative concept to Anne and asked her to think about her failure narrative. "What is your greatest self-doubt? Do you know why you have this doubt? How does it relate to your life experience?"

Anne took a few minutes to think about this question. She then explained how she had always doubted her intelligence and her judgment. She said that her parents were very demanding and always challenged her to do better. At some points in her childhood, she was afraid to bring bad news to the dinner table because she thought she might disappoint her parents. Her parents were both still alive, and the nature of her relationship with them had changed and improved, but her feelings of inadequacy remained.

I asked her another question: "Is your current desire to change jobs a function of something going on at work, or is it more about your own insecurities as you get more senior in the company and your fear of failure increases?"

Anne wasn't sure. She seemed relieved to consider this as a possibility and promised to give it further thought.

I heard back from her six months later. She had spent more time writing her failure narrative and thinking about it. She spoke to close friends about this narrative. She consulted a mental health professional. She even went back and discussed the narrative with her parents. They were surprised that their well-intentioned pushing had such an enduring and unintended impact on their daughter.

All this was cathartic and, at the same time, very challenging for Anne. It did cause her to take a fresh look at her view of her company and her future there. She realized that some of her feelings had nothing to do with the firm, but were an outgrowth of her life story.

She ultimately decided to stay put and continue her career at the company. She explained that she was now more aware that some of her bad days might be coming from her own feelings, rather than from something that was happening externally.

———————

There will be times in your life when you really aren't good enough or you will fall short. However, this is part of the journey. I have failed and fallen short many times. While I don't like it, I am learning to become more aware of trigger events that cause me to revert back to my own failure narrative. As I try to do things to become a better leader, being aware when this narrative rears its ugly head has helped me keep my balance and avoid overreacting to certain challenging situations.

Values and Boundaries

Each of us has a set of values. These comprise things like your belief in hard work, faith, love of family, helping others less fortunate, being a good person, and so on.

Values are intimately connected with "boundaries," the ethical constraints we promise ourselves we will abide by. Examples would include: I will not lie, cheat, steal, commit murder, and so on.

Why is this relevant to becoming a leader? Thinking like an owner involves weighing numerous competing considerations and constituencies. For example, we have to balance legal, ethical, and economic factors. We have to consider the interests of shareholders, customers, employees, our community, and so on. Inevitably, weighing key considerations and taking into account these various constituencies create conflicts. We can't please everyone, and so we have to make trade-offs between meeting the needs of these various groups. When this happens, we have to weigh the pros and cons of these various trade-offs and then decide what to do. How we make this decision is likely to be very much a function of *who we are* and *what we believe in*, which is heavily influenced by our values and our boundaries. Our values and boundaries shape how we weigh these trade-offs and ultimately make decisions.

Experienced leaders know that, in these situations, it helps to have a clear understanding of who you are and take ownership of the impact of your actions. When these issues come up, you are normally in the heat of battle, and there's no time to stop and explore your values and boundaries. You may be dealing with your boss, an intimidating customer, a loved one, a friend, or another outside force that is pushing you to act—*now*. And, if you aren't clear regarding who you are and what you believe, you can—in a nanosecond—make a judgment that you come to regret.

Given these realities, I recommend that you take greater responsibility for identifying your values and your ethical boundaries by taking a stab at writing them down. It may feel awkward if this is the first time you've done it. Once you have a decent draft, discuss these issues with friends and loved ones. Raise these topics with friends and employees in order to refine your thinking. Most likely, you'll feel like it was worth the effort; you will take greater responsibility for understanding your values and ethical boundaries, and those around you will appreciate the fact that you're taking greater ownership of these issues.

How Do You Feel About Lying?

Jim, a friend of mine, became a leader of a division of his company. In his first few days in the job, he held a town hall–style meeting with all his employees. At one point in the meeting, one employee asked him, "Is it OK to lie?"

Jim was a bit taken aback and quickly gave his sincere view. "I generally don't like lying," he said, "but I understand that there are times when you might shade the truth or withhold facts from a client to avoid upsetting him or her."

He continued to field questions and the meeting ended. Jim didn't give it another thought. Three months later, he got an irate call from a client who felt that one of Jim's employees had misled him. Jim was very concerned and told the client, "I'll look into this matter, but I assure you, we insist on the highest standards of ethics and do not tolerate any effort to mislead our clients."

Jim went to human resources and, together, they summoned the employee to hear his side of the story. The employee defended himself by saying, "I did exactly what you told us to do."

Jim responded emphatically: "I *never* would tell you to lie or mislead a client!" The employee held his ground, referring to Jim's initial town hall meeting and citing almost verbatim Jim's words at that meeting.

Jim felt sick. Was it possible he had given the employee the wrong idea regarding his own view of ethics and acceptable standards of behavior with clients? He gave the employee a stern warning and put him on probation. He also learned that he had better be very careful regarding his comments to employees about values and ethical boundaries. He found out the hard way that he needed to probably script answers on this issue in advance, or he might unwittingly be setting the stage for a disaster for which he would be ultimately responsible.

The tone on ethical issues and values starts at the top. That means you! You need to think about your own values and boundaries and carefully communicate these views to your people. Views on lying, diversity, bribery, and fair treatment of other human beings are issues that require thought and a firm and clear articulation—if you are a leader.

How These Two Streams Come Together

How does all this have an impact on your ability to become a leader? What does this have to do with your capacity to take ownership?

Taking ownership involves considering a variety of factors and analyzing multiple constituencies. It is highly unlikely you will be able to adequately do this by yourself. Mastering these two processes will dramatically improve your capacity to think and act as an owner.

With practice and experience, most people are able to master vision, priorities, and alignment. Where people often fall short is being open to learning about themselves on a continuing basis. Some people simply never get in the habit of being open to understanding themselves. Even those who do develop the muscles to master this process are still vulnerable to periods in which their ego gets a little too big, they tire of many of the steps described in this chapter, their key relationships might have deteriorated, or they change their perspective on key elements of their lives. The net result is that you have to constantly work at this process and fight through those stretches during which you are simply less open to examining who you are and why you do what you do.

Undertaking both of these processes in parallel makes each a bit harder at first, but over time they become easier if you are diligent about both. To work through these processes, you will need the help of others. Maybe a pat on the back, an insightful observation, or a word of encouragement from a friend or colleague is enough to do the trick. Alternatively, maybe a friend intervenes to tell you something you don't want to hear, but *need* to hear, and this discussion gets you out of a funk or helps you break through isolation.

Whatever the case, relationships are essential to this process. We will explore the challenge of developing relationships and working with others in the following chapter.

Suggested Follow-Up Steps

- *Take a stab at writing down your vision for your unit or organization (depending on your role). This should describe how you or your organization is trying to add value that is distinctive. What would the world lose if you weren't doing what you're doing?*

- *Based on this vision, what are the three or four top priorities that are essential to you adding this value? If you have more than five priorities, what are the trade-offs you would need to make in order to whittle this list down to three or four? What steps do you need to take to assess these trade-offs?*

- *How is your organization in or out of alignment with the vision and priorities you've articulated? Make two columns: "in" alignment and "out" of alignment. What do you learn from this exercise? What steps might you take to address these alignment issues?*

- *List your strengths and weaknesses relative to your current job? Are there three or four people who observe you regularly who could give you feedback on your list? Engage them and edit the list as appropriate. What do you learn from this exercise?*

- *Take a stab at writing your failure narrative. How is this narrative having an impact on your leadership, for better or for worse? In particular, how does it affect your willingness to think and act like an owner, especially your willingness to speak up or take other actions that involve some degree of risk? What surprised you about writing this narrative?*

- *Based on the exercises in the previous two items, are there steps you could take that might help you think and act more like an owner? Examples might include a greater focus on saving your money, finding a job that better matches your passions, or creating more balance in your life by increasing your emphasis on cultivating friends and family.*

CHAPTER FOUR

You Can't Do This Alone

Learning to Build Relationships and
Harness the Power of a Group

In order to fight through isolation, continue learning, and work through the processes described in chapter 3, you will need the help of others. Put another way, in order to figure out what you believe as if you were an owner, you will need to seek advice and feedback as well as the participation of others.

It's a complex world, and you will never know everything by yourself. If you are isolated from others, you will be far less likely to be able to recognize your blind spots. Other people can bring expertise and alternative perspectives that will help you see things more clearly. They can also help to overcome your fears and anxieties, and recover from the setbacks that are bound to occur.

Each of us is unique. As a result, there is enormous power in interacting and building relationships with people who can help you gain insight in order to reach your full potential.

Once you have developed a level of conviction about what should be done in a particular situation, others can offer valuable advice and bring the kinds of complementary skills that will help you develop an action plan. These people can also play critical roles in carrying out the plan of action if they feel a sense of shared ownership in the process of getting there.

Building relationships will test your ability to communicate, share, and explain your ideas. This effort will challenge you to learn to reveal your concerns, seek feedback and advice, listen with an open mind, and be flexible enough to modify your actions and views when appropriate. These are all skills that need to be cultivated and practiced.

The Risks of Isolation

As discussed in earlier chapters, leadership requires dealing with the natural risk of isolation. Too often, executives as well as aspiring leaders feel they have done well in this area—that is, until they face a critical situation where they're dealing with a difficult business issue or need advice about themselves. Too frequently, they struggle to identify a person with whom they can talk and from whom they can seek advice.

In this chapter, we'll discuss the key elements of working with others. Contrary to conventional wisdom, this effort is not about charm, dynamic speaking abilities, or your winning personality, although these qualities could certainly be helpful along the way. Instead, this is about learning to act and interact with others: disclosing your passions, sharing your ideas with others, confiding your doubts and apprehensions, asking questions of others in order to learn from them and about them, listening with an open mind, and seeking feedback and advice.

Working effectively with others involves both one-on-one and group interactions. We will discuss the need to master both of these modes of working with others, as well as how to improve your capacities to do this.

Key Elements of a Relationship

Let's start by defining the word "relationship."

It's a frequently used word, right? Despite the fact that it is so regularly used, I have found that, like "leadership," it does not have a commonly shared meaning. Most of us tend to associate relationships with affection or fondness for someone. When I ask people about their relationships, they normally talk about loved ones, or buddies, or people they generally like. The problem is that, when I ask a person who they can speak to about a sensitive issue, they all too often proceed to explain why these buddies and loved ones either don't understand them or can't be fully trusted to be discreet. In other words, they point to some reason that precludes them from confiding in their partners in those relationships.

Affection or attraction doesn't necessarily translate into mutually beneficial relationships. So let's try a more clinical definition. A relationship requires three main components:

- Mutual understanding

- Mutual trust

- Mutual respect

Note that "affection" is not part of this definition. Ironically, for all the efforts that we all put into being liked by those around us—our peers, friends, bosses, and subordinates—mutual trust, understanding, and respect turn out to be far more important to building a sustainable relationship. If you don't believe me, try giving someone a negative surprise in their year-end compensation and then explaining it with a criticism they hadn't heard from you before. You will quickly learn that all the affection and good feelings that you've worked so hard to develop will not make up for the fact that the person feels he or she can no longer trust you. He or she will gladly throw all the "how was your weekend?" or "how is your family?" or "have a nice day!" comments out the window. After enough of these traumatic experiences, I will gladly trade "being liked" for mutual understanding, trust, and respect.

If you take an inventory of your relationships that meet these three criteria, you are likely to find that your interactions with your close associates tend to have one or two of these components, but not all three. As we will see, this is a challenge that needs to be dealt with. In my experience, all three ingredients need to be present in a relationship for it to be sustainable, and for you to be able to call on that relationship in a crunch.

Relationships are essential to working through strategic issues and processes in your job. As important, they are vital to working through the challenging process of understanding yourself. This includes getting help from others in those crossroads situations where you risk derailing.

Nowhere to Turn

Frank was a forty-year-old executive with whom I had interacted on a nonprofit board. He was a rising star in his company and seemed to have a bright future. He visited me in my office in order to "catch up" and "get to know me better." After twenty-five minutes of small talk, I began to feel that it was time to wrap up the meeting. I stood up, thinking he would do the same, and got ready for us to shake hands and go our separate ways. I noticed that he didn't take my cues, but stayed resolutely in his seat. So at the risk of being rude, I mentioned that I would need to end the meeting at this point, because I had a very busy day ahead of me.

Still, Frank sat in his seat, now silent. I saw that he had something more on his mind. I realized that he had been using all the preceding small talk as a way to work up the courage to raise the issue he really wanted to raise. I sat back down and asked, "Frank, what's cooking? What's on your mind?" He paused as tears began to well up in his eyes. I got him a glass of water and asked him to forgive my rudeness and take all the time he needed to say what he wanted to say.

"I have a terrible problem," he began. "I think my current job and the company generally are good fits with my skills and my passions. I believe in what we're doing. I like my bosses and peers. However, in the last six months, I have begun to lose my temper in the office and I'm also starting to have problems in my marriage. I feel angry a lot of the time, and that anger sometimes boils over into a temper tantrum."

He continued: "Ever since I was a teenager, I've had a problem with my temper. I taught myself to be very careful about getting too emotional or letting my anger get out of control. In some cases over the past few years, I have found reasons to excuse myself from certain situations if I thought I might boil over. Luckily, this approach seemed to work—that is, until recently. I was promoted to a bigger job at work. I now have management responsibility for thirty-five people. I found that this new job carries with it frustrations that really get me upset. My bosses haven't raised this with me yet, but I think I am probably one or two incidents away from really letting my anger create a real scene at work. I am scared about what to do, and it's affecting every relationship in my life."

I asked Frank whom he had spoken with about this problem. He answered, "No one."

"Is there really no one?" I asked.

In response, he systematically ticked through every key person in his life and explained why he couldn't talk to each person. His wife, for example, was already upset with him about his long working hours and generally sour demeanor at home. His parents would think that dwelling on this type of issue was "self-indulgent," and all too typical of a coddled generation that worried too much about their feelings rather than appreciating what they had. He couldn't talk to his buddies because he felt they each had their own problems and might even be competitive with him to the point that they might be secretly pleased to hear he was having problems. His siblings wouldn't understand because, for one reason or another, they were too different from him. His clergy wouldn't understand. His bosses would judge him. His peers would use this evidence of weakness against him. The net result of all this was that, he believed, there was no one he could confide in.

He explained that he had come to see me because he knew I had been active in business, and he had also heard that I discuss these kinds of issues in my classes at Harvard.

When he finished, I asked him if he had thought about seeing a psychiatrist or psychologist. Looking surprised, he replied, "No way I'm doing that! People need to take responsibility for dealing with their problems. Seeing a shrink may be very popular these days, but sorry, as I see it, that's for people who are mentally ill."

I smiled and admitted to him that I had seen a shrink on numerous occasions over the years, and no doubt would again in the future. "Of course, people probably do think

I am a bit crazy—but seriously—I think it can be a very healthy thing to do depending on your situation."

He quickly apologized, and I told him not to worry about it.

"Frank," I continued, "the problem you describe is not as unusual as you may think. Lots of people suffer from anger issues, or depression, or anxiety. There is no shame in that—everyone has *some* kind of issue—but the real problem is the way you're dealing with it. You're isolating yourself from those who might be able to help you. For starters, I would urge you to rethink your attitude about getting help from a psychiatrist. I'd be happy to refer you to someone I trust, and I'd urge you to at least go for an initial visit. You shouldn't go through this alone. You need to develop relationships to help you address this issue. Do it now, before you do real damage to your marriage or your career."

Frank left my office without committing to anything but called about a week later and asked me to recommend a psychiatrist, which I did. I next spoke to him about three months later, when he came to visit me in my office. Right away, I could see a difference in his demeanor and the way he carried himself.

"I saw the doctor," he said. "After several visits, we discussed the idea that I suffered from severe anxiety. I agreed to try an antianxiety medication. We also talked about my entire life, including my relationships, and now I see him once a week to work through my issues. I am taking my medication and I feel much more able to control my emotions. I also realize this doesn't mean I'm a bad person; it just means I have an issue I need to address. I've talked all this through with my wife, and I feel much more optimistic and happy about our relationship."

The point of this story is not to explore the pros and cons of seeing a psychiatrist. It is about the need to develop relationships that you can turn to, so that you can share your concerns and talk through issues that you face. Frank thought he had lots of relationships, but the truth was, he didn't know how to access any of them when he needed to work through a real issue. He stumbled upon me, but henceforth he would need to put more effort into cultivating relationships based on mutual trust, understanding, and respect.

How to Build Relationships

In order to build and cultivate relationships, you need to practice three things:

- Self-disclosure

- Inquiry

- Seeking advice

Let's look at each in turn.

Self-Disclosure

Self-disclosure involves telling someone something about yourself that will help them understand you better. For example: What keeps you up at night? What are you passionate about? What are the key elements of your life story, and how do those experiences affect your actions? These are all examples of information that you can share with someone else—the kind of self-disclosure that helps the other person understand you better. It also shows that other person a great deal of respect, in the sense that you're willing to take the time and risk of telling him or her something important about yourself. And finally, this type of activity tends to build trust: by sharing this information, you are demonstrating that you trust the other person, and that person is more likely to feel that he or she can trust you.

Many people are very guarded, particularly at work, because they feel it is inappropriate to make disclosures and give others a window into their thoughts. If this is your approach, whether at work or in your private life, you are likely to find that others will reciprocate by being reluctant to disclose information to you. It's a vicious circle, and as it perpetuates itself, people find it more and more difficult to understand, respect, and trust one another. The problem may not become obvious until you get to a point when you need help or advice. When that time comes—as it does for most of us—you won't be able to build overnight the relationships you should have been investing in all along.

Of course, all this is made easier if your company has a culture that fosters relationship building. Unfortunately, in many organizations, there is a negative undercurrent, which may lead you to feel that you just can't trust your peers with confidential personal information. All it takes is one betrayal or perceived betrayal to freeze relationship-building activities. Executives need to watch for this and model desirable behavior when they are building teams and running an organization.

Inquiry

Inquiry—the second item on the list—generally refers to asking a question. In this context, I'm defining inquiry as *asking another person something about himself or herself that will help you to understand that person better.* While this sounds easy enough, the fact is that many people are terrible at framing and then asking questions of others in a way that elicits substantive information.

Think back on your own experience. How many times have you gone on business trips, or engaged in other sustained activities with people, and never asked them a single question that would open the door to learning more about them? Maybe you refrained from doing so because you thought you would annoy them, or that they would see your interest as an intrusion. It's possible that your instincts were right—but more often than not, I have found that people are (1) reluctant to share information about their lives unless they are asked, and are (2) flattered to be asked.

Think about when you have been asked about yourself. Isn't it flattering when someone tries to understand you better? Don't you take it as a sign of interest and respect? Sometimes, the hardest part is getting started. In most new relationships, you should be prepared to help get the ball rolling by learning how to ask a question.

At Harvard, we ask executives in several of our advanced programs to go out and interview five people they have known for several years. Their interviewees can include parents, spouses, bosses, and a whole host of other people they have known in their lives. By and large, they *dread* doing this. To help move the process along, we actually write up a list of questions and tell them to blame Harvard for putting them up to this task. When we debrief them after the interviews, the executives almost always report that this was the best conversation they ever had with the other person. They describe how the subject was flattered and shared much more than ever before with the interviewer. They also report that, even though they thought they knew the person, they realize now that they didn't know the person well at all. Life stories, traumas, regrets, passions—all of it comes out in these interviews. Immediately, the nature of these relationships is changed for the better. These executives laugh about their initial sense of dread and express regret that they hadn't tried this exercise many years earlier. They begin to realize that asking a question is *enormously powerful* in learning to understand someone else and in building a relationship.

Seeking Advice

Once you have learned to share information and ask questions that help you learn about the other person, you set the stage for being able to seek advice. Seeking advice also demonstrates your respect for the other person. Rather than feeling annoyed, most of us are flattered when someone seeks our opinion or asks for advice. When someone seeks my opinion, it makes me feel like I have value and that I am needed. It makes me feel better about myself.

Getting good advice can make a huge difference in your life. Giving good advice often teaches you something, as well as making you feel closer to the other person. It is ironic that, despite these benefits, many people are reluctant to seek advice because they believe they are bothering the other person or, worse, that they will appear weak to the other person.

I Never Knew You

In addition to meeting with individual leaders, I sometimes meet with senior leadership teams of companies. Once in a while, I try an exercise with the group that helps show the power of self-disclosure, inquiry, and advice. For example, I recently sat down with the fifteen senior leaders of a superb professional services firm. I asked each person in the group to turn to the person next to him or her and go through the following exercise:

1. Write down something about yourself that the person next to you probably doesn't know. Once you've written it down, disclose it to the person. Have the person do the same for you. No interruptions allowed. This takes about five minutes.

2. Write down a question you'd like to ask the other person that would, if answered, help you to

understand him or her better. Proceed to ask, listen to the answer, and then let the other person do the same with you. No interruptions allowed. This takes about six minutes.

3. Now, write down an area of deep self-doubt. Disclose this doubt to the other person and ask his or her advice on how you might address it. Next, do this once again with roles reversed. This takes seven or eight minutes.

4. What did you learn from this process?

Many of the team members explained that, even though they had known the other person for more than ten years, this was the best conversation they had ever had with that person. Pretty amazing: it took less than twenty minutes, start to finish, and it was the best conversation they ever shared.

Why? With all the hustle and chaos of running the business, they never actually took the time to reveal much in-depth information about themselves, ask questions about the other person, or seek advice about an important matter. They each recounted how they felt they now understood the other person better, felt better understood by the other, trusted the other person more, and also respected that person more.

Through further discussion, they also realized that with all the e-mails, memos, worrying about the business, and conversations on the run, they never actually took the time to do the essentials involved in building relationships. This lack of relationship building meant that team members' understanding, trust, and respect of each other had actually eroded over time. All of this had made their interactions less effective, and some members of the group were beginning to feel estranged from their peers and from the company. The lack of relationships made them feel a little less like owners and was undermining their decision-making effectiveness. This very brief exercise helped them realize that acting like owners meant putting more effort into building their relationships with each other. By doing this, they would be able to improve their mutual understanding, respect, and trust—in turn, improving their leadership effectiveness.

Seeking Feedback

All of us need feedback from those who observe us so that we can better understand our own strengths and weaknesses.

Like many of the concepts in this book, this one sounds very straightforward. Despite its simplicity, however, most people fail to do it. They view it as uncomfortable or feel that it's excessively hard work. Most people are not eager to give you criticism or constructive feedback because they fear offending you. As a result, you have to actively seek out and solicit such feedback from those who observe you in action. These people have enormously useful information to share, but only if you *ask*.

For junior people starting out in their careers, feedback normally comes down from superiors, whether they want it or not. Most companies, large and small, have systems in place to train and coach up-and-coming professionals. Nevertheless, my strong advice to young people is to take ownership of this process. You need to own your understanding of your strengths and weaknesses. In particular, you need to *understand those strengths and weaknesses as they relate to your current job or a prospective job.*

In order to do this, you will likely need to get feedback from those who observe you, and I would urge you to not wait for the year-end review to solicit this feedback. For most professionals, the year-end review is the "verdict"— that is, by that point, it's too late for you to change your behaviors in a way that would affect your compensation and promotion prospects. If in this session you are hearing significant constructive feedback for the first time, it means you have probably underperformed your potential during that year. This underperformance may be insignificant, or it may be seriously damaging to your career. I have known numerous professionals over the years who could have addressed weaknesses if they had taken proactive steps to seek and receive feedback during the year, well in advance of the year-end review.

So why don't people—especially young people with their whole professional lives ahead of them—more fully step up to this responsibility? There are various reasons:

- They'd prefer not to hear criticism. Emotionally, getting constructive feedback doesn't always feel very good. They treat feedback like going for shots at the doctor: all in all, it's better not to go unless and until someone makes you.

- They believe they are annoying people, or appearing weak or needy, by asking for feedback. Yes, asking for observations every few days would likely be way too much. However, this doesn't justify going to the other extreme of not asking at all. As discussed earlier, people are normally flattered when you ask and typically respect the fact that you're attempting to take ownership of your own skill development.

- They think of the feedback session as a way to gain favor and get connected with senior people. While there's nothing wrong with this, you want to make sure that the session is substantive—that is, make sure you are using this meeting to seek candid observations and constructive suggestions regarding what you could do better.

Of course, some people would say that one way to avoid all this discomfort is to go into your own business. If you're the boss, you can do things your own way and not worry about pleasing senior people. However, after a period of time, most people who run their own organizations begin to feel a bit isolated and start to crave a reality check and some feedback.

The Isolated Entrepreneur

The person who runs his or her own business may view getting feedback as very challenging because of a belief that there is "no one to ask." I have a steady stream of entrepreneurs come through my office, many of whom describe a challenging strategic situation in their business that requires them to examine their own leadership style. When I ask them about getting feedback from their senior leadership team, they often respond with some variation of the same story: "I am not able to get feedback. My people are intimidated." Or worse: "I don't have anyone I respect enough to give me helpful feedback."

To these people I normally say, "That doesn't make any sense. Either you need to go out and hire in order to upgrade your team, or—more likely—your team is excellent and the problem is with you. You are not treating your people with the respect they deserve. Their feedback would likely be excellent, but they're not going to offer it unless you ask. As the boss, you have far more power than you may realize. No one wants to risk speaking up because they are stuck with you as their boss; you're the person who signs their paychecks."

When entrepreneurs proactively seek advice from their subordinates, they often get great feedback and also dramatically improve their relationships with their team. This in turn encourages team members to raise issues early while there is still time to address those issues.

The Seniority Dilemma

As a person becomes more senior in his or her organization, the danger of isolation typically increases. It is very natural for professionals to seek feedback from their superiors when they are rising in an organization. At some point, though, they reach a stage at which they no longer have senior people watching them on a regular basis. At this point, the only people who *do* watch them regularly are their subordinates. While these subordinates may fill out year-end 360-degree reviews—which, of course, are useful—the boss may feel it is inappropriate and awkward to solicit feedback from them outside the formal review process. In my view, this is a mistake that needs to be corrected.

When I speak to groups of senior executives, I usually ask them to raise their hands if they are a coach to their subordinates. Normally, almost every hand in the room goes up. I then ask them to raise their hands if *they* are coached by people in the organization. Almost no hands go up.

How could this be the case? It turns out that many senior professionals feel it is not appropriate to actively seek coaching from subordinates and—at the same time— their seniors don't observe them frequently enough to offer much help. As a result, they don't have coaches. They are, to some extent, flying blind. It shouldn't be a surprise that people in this group usually develop blind spots, suffer from increasing isolation, and struggle through transitions, unless and until they correct this situation.

I urge senior professionals to learn to cultivate subordinates who can give them feedback. To do this, I encourage them to meet one-on-one with a selected group of their subordinates and ask them point blank, "Could you give me one specific piece of advice regarding how I could improve my performance?" Another approach would be to ask, "What should I stop doing? What should I start doing? What should I do more of? What should I do less of?"

In my own experience, most junior people will answer, "Nothing I can think of. Everything seems to be going fine."

At this point, you will have to follow up and say something to the effect of, "I'm really *serious*. I would like to get at least one piece of advice regarding what I could do better or differently."

By this time, beads of sweat probably are beginning to form on their forehead as they try to figure out if this is some type of perverse loyalty test they had better not flunk. Most people will be afraid to tell you what they're thinking because they're not sure that you're really sincere about wanting their feedback. So, you have to really persuade them that you *are* sincere. Eventually, in my experience, your people will summon enough courage to reluctantly describe a meaningful shortcoming in your behavior. They will likely regret their comments as soon as they have said the words. Why? They don't want to be the one to offend you by giving you a criticism that is widely shared in the organization—and probably devastatingly accurate.

Depending on how severe this feedback is, you may feel as if you've been punched in the stomach. If so, try not to show it. Simply keep your wits about you, thank the person for his or her advice, and steer the meeting to its end.

If you're like most people, you will likely follow up this meeting by calling home to talk with a loved one.

You may ask whether you're really guilty of what your subordinate just (bravely) accused you of. Typically, you'll hear a pause on the other end of the phone line and then an answer that sounds something like, "Yes that *does* sound a lot like you."

Ugh! That doesn't initially feel good! But when this happens, you immediately know that you have an issue that you need to address, and, armed with this knowledge, you will almost certainly try to address it.

As a result, a lot of good things are likely to ensue. You address the issue and hopefully improve your job performance. The junior person who raised the criticism will tell peers that you sought his or her advice, listened, and then acted on it. And finally, you will have begun to train people to not be afraid to give you feedback.

As a result, you are no longer so isolated. You now have people you have cultivated who can warn you when you're in the midst of screwing up. This has happened to me a *lot* and has helped me prevent small problems from turning into big ones.

You can't effectively lead a group if you simply rely on your formal authority to do the job. You have to empower your people and get the benefit of their insight. You have to give them a psychological ownership stake in the business and in your success. How? By turning on the switch and *asking* for advice. If you do, you will improve your self-awareness, empower your people to give you feedback, and offer employees a greater ownership stake in the enterprise. This process can greatly strengthen your team and your organization.

Recognizing the Power of a Group

If I have learned anything through teaching at Harvard, it is to recognize the power of a group. I have learned that, even though many decisions need to be made by the leader, a group will almost always come up with a better diagnosis and solution than one person acting on his or her own. Many leaders don't fully realize the enormous power right at their disposal. They may view people individually with their strengths and limitations, and fail to see that the group working together is likely to be much more powerful than the sum of its parts.

You can harness this power by assembling a diverse group of people and framing an issue for them to debate. This involves sharing enough information with members of the group that they can do in-depth analysis and then framing key questions that will draw them out. In this process, you will see the power of people listening to one another and then refining their own points of view based on what others have to say.

This is a powerful process. Have you tried it? If not, why not? Once you see this process in action, you will understand how it can help improve the effectiveness of your team and improve your ability to solve problems.

Getting the Right People in the Room

Jane was the leader of a nonprofit organization that trained teachers for secondary schools in the United States. This was a complex undertaking, as it involved assembling a staff of teachers who taught other teachers but also creating a curriculum for their training. There was also the issue of how to pay for the service; she wrestled with how much a school district would be willing to pay, as well as how big class sizes should be so that the program would be both effective and economically viable.

The program had grown dramatically as the demand for its services had increased. Jane found that growth brought both pros and cons. The good news was that revenues were increasing; the bad news was that meeting this increased demand required substantial upfront expenditures for class space and staff. Jane felt certain that there was a way to solve this timing mismatch. In her search for a solution, she met one-on-one with several people on her staff and a number of her board members. In a visit to my office, she expressed frustration that, despite those numerous meetings, she hadn't been able to figure out exactly what to do. "Maybe I have the wrong people on my team or on my board," she lamented. "I hold all these meetings and no one seems to be able to offer up a viable solution and action plan."

Jane asked me what I thought about her issue, hoping that I might be able to come up with a solution. I admitted that I would need to learn far more about the specifics of the problem, ask lots of questions, and even then, I might not come up with a brilliant solution. "Maybe the problem isn't with your people," I continued, "but with the way you're going about figuring this out. This is a complex issue—one that involves every aspect of what you do and how to finance it. My fear is that no one person knows enough to be able to analyze the situation and give you insightful advice regarding what to do. I think you might be much better off getting those same people in a room where they can all have the same information, hear each other's views, build on what they hear, and come up with a decent diagnosis and plan of action."

My specific advice to Jane was to get the right people in the room for four hours. She asked me if I'd be willing to lead parts of the meeting—in effect, treating it like a classroom. I agreed. The first segment of the meeting involved laying out the situation, doing some analysis as a group, allowing people to ask questions of each other, and generally making sure there was a shared understanding of the problem. Next, the group worked together to identify and brainstorm potential options and then identify the pros and cons of each option. After a break, they took a stab at zeroing in on the top-two options and thinking through the details of a specific game plan for each option. By the end of the meeting, it appeared that the group had come to a consensus on what to do. There was still some disagreement on a few details, but the team members agreed that they would be able to work out these issues as they got into execution. Specifically, the group decided to seek out two or three existing funders who would "bridge" the investment needed to gear up to meet additional demand.

Jane admitted to me that she was stunned at how this collection of individuals, acting as a group, was able to come up with a compelling analysis and action plan. She began to realize the power of sharing information, framing issues, letting people listen to one another, and encouraging them to build on each other's work. This process made an enormous difference in the quality of their work. With this precedent in mind, Jane began to assemble groups of people to review additional key issues. This not only gave her great advice, but also made working with the organization much more fun for both the employees and the board. People felt much more like owners, improved their level of learning and skill development, and generally enjoyed being part of a process that led to better decision making.

The Importance of Diversity

One of the most critical elements of this process is ensuring that the group is diverse.

I mean "diversity" in its broadest sense: gender, ethnicity, geographic backgrounds and cultures, functional representation, business unit representation, and different points of view. A strong leader who understands the power of the group dynamic welcomes diversity and works to create and sustain it. He or she makes sure that diverse expertise and points of view are represented, in order to develop better insight, diagnoses, solutions, and action plans.

People sometimes scoff at diversity as merely a "check the box" exercise carried out for appearance's sake. Superb leaders know that the effectiveness of working groups, such as boards of directors, is seriously impaired if they can't identify their blind spots through debate and disagreement. Of course, it takes confidence for a leader to populate his or her board or senior leadership team with people who are likely to have a different perspective or take an opposing point of view. Not surprisingly, some leaders prefer to deal with people who are similar to them, who are loyal to them personally, or who are unlikely to challenge them in debates regarding key issues facing the organization. Superb leaders overcome these insecurities and find ways to create and work with diverse groups of people. They also learn to share critical information, frame issues, and encourage debate and discussion in order to make better decisions.

The Power of Brainstorming

Brainstorming is a very specific variant of this process. In brainstorming, you are not trying to get to a solution. You are trying, instead, to relax constraints and use your imagination to develop potentially useful ideas. The key word here is "potential"—some of the ideas will not be good ones. The trick is to initially surface ideas without being overly critical so that you can ultimately identify one or more great ones.

Highly analytical people (myself included) have a bad habit of being able to explain why almost any idea *won't* work. A great idea gets shot down because someone smart convincingly pokes a hole in it. The thing is, there's *always* a really smart person around who's willing to poke holes in what might be a great idea. Brainstorming gives the analytical part of the brain a rest and gives ideas a chance to flourish.

Brainstorming forces people to suspend their judgments, free their minds, and use their creativity and imagination.

It forces people to listen with an open mind. With practice, groups can become much more creative and come up with radical and innovative ideas that they couldn't individually imagine.

The Clean Sheet of Paper, Revisited

Another variant on this process is the "clean sheet of paper" exercise. This process was mentioned as part of the alignment discussion in chapter 3. It is a good example of using the power of a diverse group to address vision, priorities, and alignment. If you learn to seek feedback and empower your people to give their views as if they were owners, if you frame questions and set loose the power of a group, if you are open to brainstorming and work at it, you should consider this exercise.

All of us have blind spots. Those of us who build businesses or nonprofits tend to get emotionally invested in what we've created and in our particular way of doing things. The problem, of course, is that *things change*. The only thing you can know for sure is that if you insist on doing things the way you've always done them, you are very likely not updating your priorities. As a result, you are probably out of alignment and are probably delivering less value to your customers.

Try asking a group of subordinates to look at what you're doing with a clean sheet of paper. That is, pretend you are starting from scratch. Are these the markets you would serve, the people you would hire, the tasks you would give them, the way you would be organized, and the leadership style you would employ? Ask them to take several weeks to consider these questions, without regard to what you're actually doing now.

After several weeks, ask them to give you their analysis and recommendations. You will very likely receive some *terrific* advice. In fact, many of the best decisions I've ever made came from doing this type of exercise. Why? Most of us tend to get too close emotionally to see problems and figure out how to address them. Also, as a leader, your views may inadvertently muzzle your people because they are hesitant to disagree with you. This exercise encourages them to disagree with you and take greater ownership of the challenges facing the organization. Try it as a way to mobilize the power of your people, train them, and punch through your own blind spots.

Learning to Work with and through Others

I said earlier in this book that leadership is a team sport. Critical to the success of a team is an ownership mind-set among its members. You will need relationships in order to create this ownership and reach your own potential. Building mutually beneficial one-to-one relationships is just a start. Learning to seek advice and feedback is a crucial follow-up step.

It is essential to build on these steps in order to harness the power of a group. Doing this will require you to improve your facilitation and listening skills. You will also need to be more proactive in sharing information so that the group can be well informed and able to understand the issues faced by you and the firm. All these techniques have one big benefit: they allow you to continue learning and to avoid isolation. You are no longer alone. Your team members have a greater stake in your success and the success of the organization. You harness the power of your people.

Why do leaders fail? Most commonly, leaders fail due to isolation and an inability to learn. Yes, you can and should learn from books and reading generally. But in addition, you *must* learn to learn from others. Relationship building and team facilitation skills will enormously improve your ability to seek feedback, learn, identify blind spots individually and for your organization, and it will make you more effective at figuring out what you believe and then acting on it in a way that adds value to others. It empowers members of your team to do the same.

If you can build these skills, you will be a potent force in your organization and in your life. And something else will happen, as well: you will be able to use these skills to be a much more potent force in the world.

Take these skills and go one step further. Make an effort to go beyond your day-to-day responsibilities and find a cause in the community and get involved. Maybe a nonprofit board or the local PTA would be potential options for you. There are myriad problems facing your community and the world; use your talents to make an impact on one of them.

These activities are rewarding in and of themselves; they also give you an opportunity to exercise new muscles in terms of relationship development and working with groups. They will open your eyes more fully to the power of a group of people working together and acting like owners. Once you have experienced this, you will want to find new opportunities to leverage the power of a group.

Suggested Follow-Up Steps

- *Make a list of people in your life with whom you have a relationship as defined in this chapter—that is, mutual trust, mutual understanding, and mutual respect.*

- *With whom do you practice self-disclosure, inquiry, and seeking advice? If the list is short, why?*

- *Make a list of subordinates from whom you seek feedback. If the list is short, why?*

- *What actions could you take to improve the number and nature of your relationships?*

- *Can you bring to mind an incident in which you effectively muzzled the potential contributions of a subordinate or a colleague? If so, how would you handle that incident differently today?*

- *Are there people in your organization whom you consider isolated? How do they interact with others, including you? How might their behaviors contribute to their isolation? Now ask yourself: do I also practice some of these isolating behaviors?*

CHAPTER FIVE

The Ownership Path as a Lifelong Journey

Taking Steps and Making Use of Tools That Will Help You Become a Better Leader

Throughout this book, I have tried to underscore the point that leadership is not a destination. It is not a state of being. It is not something either you're born with or you're not.

Leadership is not about the position you hold; it's about the actions you take. It's about having an ownership mindset. Leadership is about what you do, rather than who you are. It must be learned and relearned. It requires hard work and persistence. It is analogous to losing weight or getting in shape; it is a regimen of work that you never finish. It is a lifelong effort to adapt to transitions and—in the process—to improve.

As I've said in earlier chapters, all this must start with the proper attitude and mind-set. In particular, you have to reject the notion that leadership is a magical state of being that can't be learned. Instead, you have to resolve to begin to work at it today and every day. To go down this road, you will probably need to reexamine your previous assumptions about the world and your own life. The most important mind-set adjustment you'll need to make is to more fully accept that your life is your own, and that you have to actively take responsibility for it.

Take Ownership of Your Life

Once again, *you are responsible for your life*. You are the owner of what you do and of the decisions that you make. Do you believe that and, if so, do you act accordingly? This means working consistently on a series of steps that will improve your leadership abilities.

What's the best way to begin this process? Previous chapters of this book laid out a series of suggested steps and actions intended to help you improve your leadership. Rather than trying to adopt several of these steps immediately, many people find that it is more realistic to make an initial commitment to a manageable number of first steps in order to get rolling.

This chapter will discuss your mind-set and a menu of potential actions that will help you get started. I would urge you, as you read this chapter, to write down three to five actions that you would be willing to commit to pursuing over the next few weeks. After you have taken these first steps, I would suggest that you then go deeper and add additional actions that will broaden your repertoire.

Write Down Strengths and Weaknesses

Acting like the owner of your life starts with being able to write down your strengths and weaknesses. This is something you need to work on today, tomorrow, and for the rest of your life. Why? You will change, the world will change, your job will change, and the nature of various industries and sectors will change. In the context of all this change, you need to regularly reassess your skills. As discussed in chapter 3, this doesn't mean you need to somehow overcome each of your significant weaknesses; it *does* mean that you need to be aware of them. Armed with this awareness, you can choose to work on some of these weaknesses, if meaningful improvement is realistic and important to your performance. On other weaknesses, you may need to more actively seek help from others with complementary skills in order to improve your leadership effectiveness.

Most people I know are unable to perform this strengths-weaknesses assessment accurately. Why? Understanding your strengths and weaknesses is challenging because it requires you to solicit feedback from those who observe you. All of us have blind spots that limit our ability to accurately assess ourselves. There are certain aspects of our behavior that we simply can't see, even though everyone around us may see them very clearly.

As a consequence, to assess your strengths and weaknesses, you need to cultivate people who observe you.

This means proactively encouraging them to tell you things you may not want to hear, but need to hear. This takes a lot of emotional strength on your part and will require some persuasion. No one wants to offend you, especially if you supervise them. Unless you proactively ask them, people will prefer to keep quiet about your shortcomings.

As we discussed in the previous chapter, you will need to sit down with people one-on-one and ask them the following question: "Can you give me one or two things I could do to improve?" You'll have to convince them—through your tone and demeanor—that you really want their help. If their feedback rings true, you'll need to take steps to address it.

As a result of this, you will improve. The person who gave you the feedback will feel good about helping you. Over time, you will train people who observe you to be willing to give you feedback. You will be less isolated and open the door to learning more about your skills. I urge you to start the process of actively seeking feedback; it will benefit you for the rest of your life.

Dream Your Dream

Taking responsibility means not being afraid to dream your dream. Again, I am talking about *your* dream, not your parents' dream, not your friend's dream, not what's socially cool, but *your* dream. Your dream may seem weird by conventional standards. It may elicit disapproval from friends or loved ones. At the same time, it might well turn out to be *fantastic*.

Dreaming your dream is not a selfish indulgence. In fact, it is essential to performing at a high level. As discussed earlier in this book, passion is the rocket fuel that drives high performance. It is hard to perform at a high level for a sustained period of time without a passion for at least some key elements of your job. Only you can answer the question of what ignites your passions.

Many people have gone so many years without dreaming about what they love that they become rusty. Put another way, they haven't used their imagination and exercised their creative muscles in quite some time. To reawaken their passions, they need to start *exercising* those muscles.

One way to jump-start this effort is to think about a time in your life when you were at your best—when you *shined*. You loved what you were doing and it felt great. What were you doing? What were the elements of the situation that caused you to love it and perform at a high level? What can you learn from this experience regarding what you might love? What were the elements or the task or the mission or the situation that brought out your best?

Try this exercise. Dreaming your dream is central to identifying your passions and excelling. It is part of taking ownership of your life. Don't be afraid to dream your dream.

Beware of Conventional Wisdom

As you dream your dream, beware of conventional wisdom.

Conventional wisdom consists of the things that "everyone knows" to be true. If you're going to figure out what you believe as a leader, you are going to have to learn to avoid being unduly influenced by conventional wisdom. This "wisdom" is often wrong or out of date, and it doesn't take into account the specifics of your situation.

When I was graduating from college, there were a number of things that everyone "knew" to be true about the future. If you wanted to get ahead, you had to be mindful of those seemingly universal truths. For example:

- Japan was expected to dominate the world for the rest of our lives. Having emerged after World War II as an industrial powerhouse, and having overtaken the United States in terms of manufacturing prowess and management practices, Japan was expected to dominate commerce for our lifetimes. If you wanted to be a successful businessperson someday, you had damn well better begin studying Japanese business practices and, even better, learn Japanese.

- The encyclopedia was the most valuable repository of information in the world. If you wanted to stay abreast of the latest knowledge—and have easy access to it—you needed to protect that encyclopedia and start budgeting for the day when you'd have to shell out big money to update it with new editions.

- Every major city had at least one morning and one afternoon newspaper—sometimes with extra editions—that were a primary way to keep abreast of the news (in addition to TV and radio, of course). This business model was expected to continue into the foreseeable future.

- High inflation was a permanent fact of life in the United States. Interest rates were expected to remain well over 10 percent indefinitely. It was hard to imagine that any of us would ever be able to get a home mortgage with a rate below 10 percent.

- Medical doctors had it made. Medicine was a lucrative and high-status profession, and it was expected to always stay that way.

Of course, this list could go on and on. The point is that the world changes in ways that are difficult, even impossible, to foresee. Just because everyone knows that something is true doesn't mean it will continue to be true and certainly doesn't mean that it's true with regard to you.

You are unique in terms of your skills, passions, values, and life story. Conventional wisdom tends to be applied with a broad brush, as if everyone were the same. But everyone is *not* the same. You've got to do your own analysis and thinking that fits your unique qualities and the essence of who you are. Learn to get opinions, but also think for yourself. A saying that I often heard growing up in Kansas makes the point: "How many legs does a cow have if you call its tail a leg?" The answer is *four*: just because you call a tail a leg doesn't make it a leg.

In other words, don't be afraid to challenge assumptions everyone knows to be true. And always keep in mind that what's right for someone else may not be the right thing for you.

Make a Leap of Faith

Assume that justice will ultimately prevail. Most of us go through experiences in our lives in which we believe we were treated unfairly. What's your version of this experience? Maybe you didn't get the promotion you expected or the compensation you deserved. Maybe you were judged unfairly by someone else.

What lessons did you learn from these experiences? Maybe you concluded that people can't be trusted, and that you have to look out for yourself. Maybe you learned that it was dangerous to confide in others or to help others, and as result, you are reluctant to seek advice, give advice, or empower others. Whatever your experience, the question is: how are these lessons helping or undermining your ability to be a leader and follow many of prescriptions in this book?

The fact is, at any point in time, justice may *not* prevail. But over the long run, it normally does prevail. Are you letting a setback or an injustice throw you off your game? If so, you may be behaving in a way that undermines your own natural abilities. In particular, you may be undermining your ability to figure out what you believe and step up to act in a way that adds value to others.

Try making a leap of faith. Assume that justice will prevail. See how it helps you act more like a leader and develop an ownership mind-set.

Focus on Adding Value to Others

This brings us back to another central theme of this book: leadership is about adding value to others. It involves taking ownership of the impact of your actions on your key constituencies: customers, shareholders, employees, your community, the environment, and so on.

"Value" can mean selling a good or service that satisfies a need of a customer or a client. It can mean performing a function that helps the community. It can mean protecting someone from being hurt, physically or emotionally, or from suffering some other sort of damage.

In my experience, money and other positive outcomes should not be ends in and of themselves; they come as a result of adding value over a sustained period of time. Put differently, even if your primary desire is money, status, power, or some other extrinsic motivator, the best way to achieve these outcomes is to focus on adding value consistently, over time.

Of course, this approach also requires a leap of faith. Superb business leaders tend to come to this realization sometime during their careers, understanding that they need to focus their efforts on adding value that is distinctive in order to help their organizations succeed. On the other hand, many experienced leaders become skeptical or lose sight of this way of thinking. Due to their own life experiences, they begin to doubt the premise of this assertion. Their doubt is exacerbated when they see enormous sums of money being made in certain industries. They ask, "How does *that* leader, or *that* business, add value to anyone?"

I think if they look more closely, and over a longer time horizon, they will see that either the leaders or organizations in question add more value than it appears or, if they don't, their success will prove short-lived.

Long-Term versus Short-Term Profitability

Chen Lee ran a midsized distribution company in Asia. Her firm started out as the primary distribution company for a beverage manufacturer. Over a period of years, she expanded her product line to include additional food items that were sold through retail grocery and other retail food outlets. But as the firm got bigger and technology evolved, Chen Lee found her margins were eroding.

She addressed this shrinkage by cutting costs, using technology to run more efficiently, and pruning less profitable product lines. Nevertheless, the erosion continued. When I visited her in Asia, she explained why cutting costs was so important: "The bottom line is why we're here. My dream is to build a big distributorship and set records for profitability."

When I asked about her vision for the business, she responded, "I want to be the most profitable distributor in our industry in Asia." I suggested that was a vision about her, rather than a vision of how the business added value. I asked her how she added value that was distinctive.

In response, she simply repeated her previous statement about profitability.

As we discussed the business, I asked Chen Lee to tell me why manufacturers and retailers did business with her firm. She talked about breadth of selection, customer service, and speed of delivery. I asked how her recent moves had an impact on this value. "It hurts our value proposition," she admitted, "but we have no choice. We've got to make our numbers."

Chen Lee asked for my reaction to her approach. I told her that I thought she had it all backward. I asserted that adding value leads to more revenue and profits—over a period of time. If the client isn't willing to pay for your service or isn't willing to pay sufficiently for you to make a decent profit, you need to go back and rethink your value proposition and provide services the client does value and is willing to pay for.

I encouraged Chen Lee to go out and interview ten or fifteen of her customers and discuss these issues. To her credit, she did this quickly and discovered some surprising things. Customers wanted *more* breadth from her company, in terms of product offerings. In fact, she learned that her customers were cutting down their overall number of distributors and sticking with those that offered more full service. She also learned that her customer service had been eroding for several years, and the recent cost cuts simply accelerated that deterioration. Customers made clear that they were willing to pay fair prices in return for breadth of offerings and good service—in other words, exactly the opposite direction from the one Chen Lee had chosen.

Chen Lee went back to her company and made changes to address these two issues. Within two years, her margins had returned to higher levels and sales were growing. As a result of this searing experience, she changed her orientation in running the business. In particular, she decided that her focus needed to be, first, on adding value, and that profitability goals would be met as a by-product of this focus.

A focus on adding value has another great benefit: it is more likely to bring out the best work of you and your employees. Aspiring to add value ignites your passion and makes you more likely to shine. As wonderful as money, power, status, and other visible manifestations of success may seem to you, they will remain elusive unless you are passionate about the day-to-day content and purpose of your work.

A Passion for Making a Difference

I was visited by Fred, a sixty-eight-year-old ex-CEO of a *Fortune* 500 company. Fred was in great health and intellectually very active. He had been careful to save for his retirement and, as a result, was well situated financially. Despite this, he was deeply depressed.

"Since I stepped down as CEO," he told me, "the silence has been deafening. Yes, people have been very gracious and polite. The new CEO, who I groomed as my successor, has made clear to me that he'd like to talk, but only every once in a while. Otherwise, he wants me to stay away from the company. I never was very active in nonprofit activities, although I always chaired the local United Way campaign. I never saw how nonprofit activities would help my career or my company. I guess I always assumed that my business career would naturally morph into a great post-business career. But now I'm not really sure about my skills, what I'm interested in, or how I can help anyone else. How do I get myself back to being relevant in the world?"

I asked Fred to think about what cause—in his town or in the world—he had a passion for addressing. He responded, "I need to think about that, because I honestly don't know. My analysis was always about what would help my career, not how to solve the problems of the world. I'm embarrassed to admit that I thought that was the role of government or charities—not my role."

I challenged Fred to really think about how he could add value without worrying about what was in it for him. "You have enormous talent that I'm sure could make a big impact," I said. "But, you need to do some work on understanding what you might have a passion for and what's important to you. Maybe you need to defrost a bit and start taking a much deeper look at the problems of the world. Take a few months, read more broadly, talk to people, and so on. Then, let's talk again."

Fred came back three months later. He was still depressed, but he had begun to realize that he had lived a somewhat isolated existence over the previous few decades. He had not been looking beyond his job and his business—wearing blinders professionally and focusing on the immediate needs of his family. He began to see that, if he was going to make more out of the rest of his life, he needed to started looking outward much more and figure out where he could add value—to others.

Over time, he explored several areas and allowed himself to *dream*—specifically, about adding value based on his passions. He ultimately became very actively involved as a volunteer in a children's literacy program. This started off as spending one day a week reading to a grade-school child during his lunch hour. He then contributed money to the program. He was then asked to join the board. After two years as a board member, he became the chairman of the board. About two years later, a magazine was doing an article on "second acts" of CEOs. Fred was described as a "success story" based on his work chairing this board, as well as two or three other involvements he had developed.

At one point, Fred made an interesting comment to me. "I thought I would be remembered for my work as CEO," he said. "I now believe I am more likely to be remembered for my work in the nonprofit world. It's funny how my thinking on life has changed. I realize that being an owner doesn't need to mean owning a financial stake. It's a mind-set that involves taking responsibility for the impact of what I do. I now see all sorts of areas where I can add value and make a difference in the world. I now feel like I have an ownership stake in what happens in this world. Once again, I'm excited about the future!"

Be Open to Learning

In chapter 2, we explored reasons why leaders fail. One such reason was the failure to be open to learning.

Other reasons included an inability to be authentic as well as a discomfort with being vulnerable enough to ask questions.

As simple as this all sounds, it is often easier said than done. Why don't people ask questions and keep learning? The things that tend to get in the way include ego, insecurities, and mental models of leadership. How much are you able to be authentic and admit what you do and don't know?

A good test of this willingness is your ability to say the following phrases:

- I was wrong.

- I made a mistake.

- I've changed my mind.

- I don't know.

- I'm sorry.

- I'd like to ask your advice.

How many of these phrases do you say, at least every once in a while? Are you so infallible—or so proud—that you can't bring yourself to admit you've made a mistake, or that you don't know something, or that you've changed your mind?

Many people think that using one of these phrases is a sign of weakness or will cause people to think less of them. In fact, the opposite is true: these phrases help you stop digging a hole deeper when you've made a mistake, and they invite the people around you to help you stop digging and climb out of that hole.

Using these phrases also sets a tone that encourages your people to admit mistakes, ask for help, and generally confront issues. This makes it more likely that issues and problems will be raised and addressed in a timely manner.

Stop Digging and Start Learning

Monica ran her own retail store. She was an excellent merchant and judge of fashion trends. She considered herself an accomplished businessperson, as evidenced by her ability to open and run a store that was highly profitable.

She had started the store with a partner who handled accounting, finance, and the rest of the business side of running the store. Monica always felt a little self-conscious when meetings with her partner turned to financial topics. Privately, she felt she really didn't understand what her partner was talking about. She dealt with this insecurity by acting as if she understood these topics and bristled when her partner went in depth into some of these aspects. "I know that. You don't need to explain this to me," she would say on occasion.

Monica's partner ultimately moved with her family to another city and, as a result, the partnership dissolved; Monica became the 100 percent owner of the business. At this point, she believed she could handle both roles—in part by relying more on the business's outside accountant—and therefore made no moves to bring in additional financially oriented help.

I met Monica in the Owner/President Management program at Harvard Business School, during which she came to my office to review the state of her business. She explained how profitability had slumped, and how she was taking decisive action to cut costs and trim employee hours. She wondered whether part of the problem was the store location and explained that she had begun looking at alternative locations in her city that might have more customer traffic and be a more convenient destination for her customers.

I asked her to explain her diagnosis and action plan. Monica attempted to take me through the analysis, but at its end, I had to admit I still couldn't understand what she was saying. She painfully struggled to explain her financials, pinpoint where she was and wasn't making money, and connect this back to her tactical moves.

After several rounds of this, I asked, "Monica, who is helping you with these financial matters? You have several great strengths, but is financial acumen one of them?"

She answered very assertively, "I am very comfortable with these matters. I definitely have sufficient help. Maybe you don't understand retail very well, which would explain why I can't get this across to you."

"Fair enough," I said. But I explained that, if I was going to help her any further, she was going to have to take the time to honestly figure out and write down her strengths and weaknesses. And, by the way—I told her—there's no shame in having weaknesses. The truth is, we all have them. The real challenge is to figure out what they are and how to compensate for them.

To get at this challenge, I encouraged Monica to interview four or five people who knew her in the work setting. I cautioned her not to get angry if these people turned out to be honest enough to tell her she had a weakness; after all, that reaction would shut them down and defeat the purpose of this exercise. She had to keep an open mind on this subject.

She called me several weeks later to talk. She complained that business was still slumping, and she hadn't figured out how to address the problem. I asked her if she had done the strengths and weaknesses exercise. Impatiently, she said that she had not. "We're not running a school here. This is a business and we're having problems. I need to focus!" she answered.

I was sympathetic but pushed her again, and told her that until she did this exercise, she would be flying blind regarding how to arrest this decline.

"I get what you're doing," she replied. "You want me to admit that I'm no good at financial analysis and that I need help. Truthfully, I'm a little hurt that you think this about me. I'm a businessperson, not just some fashion-merchandising geek!"

Three months later, Monica called me again. This time, it was a different story. She said that she finally had gotten so exasperated that she forced herself to get some feedback from her former partner. Without going through the blow-by-blow, it was clear that she had begun to realize that she was overly defensive about her financial capabilities, that this defensiveness was hurting her ability to deal with this situation, and that it might be a relief to admit that she needed help. Based on the feedback from her former partner, she decided to hire a local person with strong analytical skills to work with her twenty hours a week. The person she hired examined her business results and helped her think through her options. Already, it had proven an eye-opening experience. She learned that a portion of her merchandise was, after markdowns, actually losing money, and that she was under-inventoried on several categories of fast-moving goods. She also figured out that her former partner had been in the habit of spotting these kinds of problems and diplomatically addressing them without bothering Monica.

Right off the bat, she changed her approach to ordering and inventory management. She hired additional store staff and—to her surprise—found that her profitability began to increase. She stopped thinking about changing store locations.

Sometimes when I'm in her town, we get together for coffee. Invariably, we wind up having a good laugh over this story. We commend each other for our single-mindedness, and we agree that it's OK to have a weakness as long as you acknowledge it and stay open to learning. Ironically, I sometimes use her as a coach to help me identify my own blind spots. She's become pretty darn good at it and has helped me face up to some of my own shortcomings.

Make Use of Tools That Create Greater Ownership

Assuming that you're determined to make yourself a better leader, what are some of the tools you can use to help you get there? Let me suggest a few.

Create a Case

Very frequently, the big debates we have in our personal and professional lives are not actually about a difference of opinion. They are, instead, about a difference in our respective understanding of the facts. Each person involved in the situation has different assumptions about the underlying facts. Based on this difference in understanding, each has a different analysis of the situation, a different view of the options, and a different opinion about the most appropriate plan of action.

Very often, members of the group mistakenly assume they are on the same page regarding the basic facts, when they most certainly are not. This phenomenon is most starkly presented on television and radio when two opposing voices debate an issue. It is clear that they disagree on what should be done. But if you listen carefully, you may discover that they don't agree on the basic facts of the case, which would explain why they don't agree on anything else.

If you think this might be happening to you—if you find yourself getting involved in passionate arguments that seem to go nowhere—try the following experiment. Lay out the facts of the situation in a five- or six-page document (that is, *briefly*). If possible, interview all the parties involved to clarify and make sure you have a shared understanding of the facts. On those points where there's a legitimate dispute about the facts, lay that out explicitly in the document, so people are able to understand the range of interpretations. Then ask members of the group to read the document in advance and come to a meeting prepared to debate and discuss the issues.

I think you'll find that you will very quickly get to a shared agreement on the facts of the situation, develop a general consensus on the diagnosis, and be able to articulate the different points of view. The group can then dig deeper into the reasons for those differences. Each participant is forced to explain his or her point of view based on facts, and each learns from others in the discussion. As a result, the group is very likely to forge a coherent consensus—or at least a pretty tight range of views—that can form the basis for discussing action steps on a way to move forward.

This technique allows you to harness the power of a diverse group and gives members the opportunity to think like owners. It is also a great skills-development exercise for team members and dramatically improves group effectiveness. Learn to start with laying out the facts and getting a shared understanding when you are facing a challenging issue. Make sure you are arguing over *issues* rather than a misunderstanding regarding the basic facts.

Learn to Ask "Framing Questions"

Most of us can ask questions that elicit a simple yes or no answer. Some of us can ask the kinds of questions that surface useful information or help elicit someone's opinion on a relatively narrow matter.

Asking a framing question is different. It requires substantially more thought and preparation, because it needs to be broad enough to get a stream of discussion going. A framing question can be used to elicit a diagnosis: "What's the problem here?" "Is this a crisis—and if so, why?" "Who are the key constituencies in this situation?" "What's going on in the industry and overall economy that might explain what's happening?"

To be effective, framing questions should cause participants to take a fresh look at a situation or look at it from a slightly different perspective. For example, the CEO of a technology company prided himself on regularly asking his employees for ways the company could improve its operations. He complained to me that he normally got superficial answers and advice, and his people interpreted the questions as rhetorical. He asked whether there was a problem with the way he was soliciting this advice. I suggested that he block out ninety minutes and ask an assembled group three types of framing questions that were intended to spur their thinking from a slightly different perspective:

- Why do you work here? What's great about this company? What is your dream for this company? (30 minutes of discussion)

- What do you hate about working here? What are we doing that gets us out of alignment and keeps us from achieving your dream for the company? (30 minutes)

- Can you suggest one specific action for how we can deal with these issues and improve our ability to help reach our dream for this firm? (30 minutes)

He was amazed with the quality of the discussion and the terrific suggestions he received, and wound up implementing several of the suggestions. Why was this discussion so effective? He had created a frame for the advice that forced the group to think more deeply. It caused the group members to step back and think about their hopes and aspirations as well as what was bothering them. It also gave them a framework for expressing their views.

There are various types of framing questions. They are intended to get participants to share their views, learn from each other, push their own thinking further and deeper, understand each other better, and operate more effectively as a unit. As you try different questions, you'll learn which are most effective in generating a useful discussion. This type of framing exercise helps you get more from your people and helps them act more like owners.

Most important, it gives you an opportunity to learn from your people.

Learn to Listen

Most of us think we spend the majority of our time listening, rather than talking. That may or may not be true, but even when it *is* true, we may not be listening very well. There is a huge difference between passively hearing and actually *listening*.

Listening is an active exercise. It is exhausting. It requires concentration. It is a skill that must be learned and practiced. The good news is that the more you do it, the better you get. Most people understand that practice makes perfect when it comes to speaking, but for some reason, when it comes to listening, they don't get it. For a leader, speaking effectively is important, but listening effectively may be *more* important.

It has often struck me that the biggest change in many of the executives who come to our courses at Harvard is the dramatic improvement in their listening skills. Yes, they learn content, theory, and frameworks; they read cases, share their views, and so on. But the most transformative change is their improved ability to actively listen.

So find a way to practice listening. At first, you may not be able to actively listen to another person for very long without losing your concentration. Don't be discouraged. It's like getting in physical shape: With practice, your endurance will improve. Think about when you listen best and try to re-create those circumstances as you practice listening.

Use Mental Models That Create an Ownership Mind-Set

I have referred to this technique at several points in this book. It's a technique whereby you clarify your thinking by relaxing a constraint and thinking about the implications. For example: "If you had a huge amount of money, what would you do?" "If you assumed you were in charge, what would you do?" "If you only had two years to live, what would you do?" "If you weren't afraid of upsetting the boss, what would you do?" "If you knew that your efforts would succeed, where would you apply your energies?" "If you lengthened the time frame from six months to five years, how would that affect your decision?"

These approaches create more psychological ownership. They can be enormously powerful tools for an individual, and they can also help a group focus its thinking. They help people screen out peer pressure, money pressure, irrelevant considerations, and their own insecurities.

In your continuing effort to figure out what you truly believe, mental models can unleash your mind, identify what's really most important to you, and help you develop conviction about a point of view.

Do Exercises

In the preceding chapters, you've been exposed to a series of exercises: self-disclosure, inquiry, seeking advice, clean sheet of paper, and so on. As you've certainly realized by now, I am a big fan of these approaches. Why? They can help create framing questions that enable you and your organization to think more clearly, and help the people around you understand each other—and you—more fully.

Develop an Inventory of Your Relationships and Consider Creating a Support Group

Building on the issues discussed in chapter 4, take an inventory of your relationships and—based on that inventory—consider creating a support group.

The support group is a resource described by my Harvard Business School colleague Bill George, in his book *True North*.[1] It is designed to give you a group of people with whom you can confide, share confidential information, discuss issues you face, and generally be authentic. We use these groups in every session of our course, "The Authentic Leader." We put executives into groups with five peers and establish a meeting structure, an agenda, rotating discussion leadership, and other parameters. Group members sign an agreement to keep matters confidential, to be on time, to share, and to keep mobile devices stored for the duration of the discussion. These sessions have been enormously successful and are usually a highlight of the course.

Most executives who participate in this process come to realize the power of the support group. It is so effective that many try to replicate this resource when they go back home.

Give and Receive Feedback

Let's assume that you've taken the steps I've discussed up to this point, maybe even going so far as to create a support group. If so, I urge you to use this new resource to practice giving and receiving feedback. Positive feedback is just as important as negative (or constructive) feedback.

A core message of this book is that most of us have blind spots. We don't understand how great we are at certain things, and we don't realize how weak we are in other areas. Getting feedback allows us to see these blind spots and sets us on the road to understanding ourselves better.

Most of us also need to do a better job at *giving* feedback. This skill can help you say what you want, support someone else, and help repair or maintain a relationship. How many times have you written someone off because you didn't want to confront him or her about something he or she was doing that you found annoying? The truth is, some amount of confrontation is healthy in a relationship. Practicing giving feedback can help you do this.

Keep a Journal

Amid the chaos of everyday life, you need time to think and reflect. Sometimes, in the wake of an important experience, getting perspective requires that you step back and write down your observations. For this reason, I recommend keeping a journal. Blocking out time to write down your thoughts can be an extremely constructive habit.

Documenting your thoughts is valuable in real time. It may also be valuable as your thinking gets reframed with the passage of time. Keeping a journal helps you gain perspective. It helps you figure out what you believe and, ultimately, helps you take action. It can also help you develop your thinking regarding how you want to add value to others.

Create Space for Face-to-Face Communication

Given the time pressures and chaos of our daily lives, we can fail to carve out sufficient time and space for face-to-face interactions. Yes, networking with people may be very useful, but it can't take the place of meeting with someone face-to-face in order to discuss a real problem. In-person interaction allows you to see the other person's facial expression, body language, and so on.

Humans are social animals. We need to connect with each other. Failure to do so may make it harder for you to develop relationships, and over time, it may lead to the kinds of misunderstandings that can undermine your ability to work with and through others.

Interview People

Sometimes, in order to really learn about someone else, it is highly effective to interview him or her. Yes, this may seem like a stilted thing to do, and it may make you feel awkward. My experience, though, is that it can be a terrific experience. It is an obvious extension of learning to ask questions of someone that will help you to understand him or her better. Very often, it will help you realize that there is much you don't know about someone else.

If you are rusty at this skill, try interviewing someone you know. Take this exercise seriously: prepare questions in advance, arrange a reasonably private setting for the conversation, make sure you block out sufficient time, turn off your cell phone, and so on. This exercise will help you to improve your ability to learn about others and help you build relationships.

Read Newspapers, Magazines, and Books, and See Movies

Try to stay well informed on current events and aware of popular culture. This will help you be up to date on what's going on in the world, understand emerging trends, relate to others, and ultimately figure out what you believe. Popular culture, macro trends, and other issues shape your point of view and create important context for figuring out how to take action and how to add value to others.

The World Needs You

Leadership is about taking ownership. It's about seeing an issue and not waiting for someone else to address it. It's about your mind-set. Yes, adopting an ownership mind-set is very likely to create some stress and agitation. In some ways, it's far easier for you to leave the big problems to someone else. However, the world needs you. Of course, some problems may be of such size and scope that they are unrealistic for you to tackle. You have to calibrate your efforts to actions that have a chance of making a difference. This starts with finding an issue you care about, where you can realistically make a positive impact. This issue may relate to you, your family, organization, town, state, or country. The point is that you can make a difference, and the more you practice tackling an issue, the better you are likely to become at making a difference.

Think about the challenges in the world that you care about. Find a way to get involved. Join a nonprofit board or help someone who could benefit from your judgment and skills. Your involvement will help that organization or that individual. It will also help you to further develop your leadership skills.

The problems of the world aren't going to be solved by someone else. If they're going to be solved, they will have to be addressed by someone like you.

This book is intended to get you started along a path of developing your leadership capabilities. I emphasize that it's a *start*. I hope the impact of this book will be measured not by where you are now, but where you will be one, five, or ten years from now, and beyond.

I hope that some of the approaches discussed here resonate with you. I also hope that you'll develop your own approaches. The question is, *are you willing to engage in this effort and commit to continuing into the future?*

Of course, this regimen and your activities must be adapted to who you are. This includes your values and ethical boundaries. It also has to be adapted to where you are now, your family obligations, financial situation, and other characteristics of your life.

However you decide to use your talents, if you are true to your values, principles, and who you are, if you are motivated to keep learning and apply your skills and energy with determination, and if you never compromise your integrity in hopes of short-term success, I am confident that you will make a real impact.

If you follow this approach, I don't know how much money, power, or status you'll ultimately have. But I do believe you will find a path to leading in your own distinctive way. More importantly, I think you will *feel* like a big success, and that will make all the difference.

Suggested Follow-Up Steps

- *Write down three to five steps you plan to take over the next few weeks.*

- *Discuss these steps with a friend or close associate.*

- *Make a commitment to yourself to work on these steps.*

Essentials of What You Really Need to Lead

The Ownership Mind-Set
(Chapter 1)

- What do you believe?
- Do you act on your beliefs?
- Do you focus on adding value to others?
- Do you create an environment that encourages an ownership mind-set?

Tackling the Challenges of Leadership
(Chapter 2)

- Are you able to ask questions?
- Are you open to learning?
- Can you fight through isolation?
- Can you overcome discomfort of feeling vulnerable?

Mastering the Essential Processes of Leadership
(Chapter 3)

- Vision, priorities, and alignment
- Understanding yourself
  - Strengths and weaknesses
  - Passions
  - Values and ethical boundaries
  - Your story

You Can't Do This Alone
(Chapter 4)

- Establish mutual understanding, trust, and respect
- Practice self-disclosure, inquiry, and seeking advice
- Harness the power of a group

The Ownership Path as a Lifelong Journey
(Chapter 5)

- Make a commitment to the process
- Use key tools
  - Create a case
  - Ask framing questions
  - Actively listen to others
  - Use mental models
  - Do ownership exercises
  - Create a support group
  - Give and receive feedback
  - Keep a journal
  - Emphasize face-to-face communication
  - Interview people

A Leadership Reading List

Arbinger Institute. *Leadership and Self-Deception*. San Francisco: Berrett-Koehler, 2010.

Bazerman, Max H., and Ann E. Tenbrunsel. *Blind Spots: Why We Fail to Do What's Right and What to Do About It*. Princeton, NJ: Princeton University Press, 2011.

Beer, Michael, and Flemming Norregren et al. *Higher Ambition: How Great Leaders Create Economic and Social Value*. Boston: Harvard Business Review Press, 2011.

Bennis, Warren G., and Robert J. Thomas. "Crucibles of Leadership." *Harvard Business Review*, September 2002.

Bower, Joseph L. *The CEO Within*. Boston: Harvard Business School Publishing, 2007.

Cohn, J. M., Rakesh Khurana, and Laura Reeves. "Growing Talent as if Your Business Depended on It." *Harvard Business Review*, October 2005.

Collins, Jim. *Good to Great*. New York: HarperCollins Publishers, 2001.

Collins, Jim, and Morten T. Hansen. *Great by Choice*. New York: HarperCollins Publishers, 2011.

Collins, James C., and Jerry I. Porras. "Building Your Company's Vision." *Harvard Business Review*, September–October 1996.

Conger, J., and K. Xin. "Voices from the Field: Trends in Executive Education Among Global Corporations." *Journal of Management Education* 24, no. 1 (2000): 73–101.

Covey, Stephen R. *The 7 Habits of Highly Effective People: Restoring the Character Ethic.* New York: Simon and Schuster, 1989.

DeLong, Thomas J. *Flying Without a Net*. Boston: Harvard Business Review Press, 2011.

Drucker, Peter. *The Essential Drucker.* New York: HarperCollins, 2001.

Eakin, John Paul. *Living Autobiographically: How We Create Identity in Narrative.* Ithaca, NY: Cornell University Press, 2008 .

Edmondson, Amy. "Psychological Safety and Learning Behavior in Work Teams." *Administrative Science Quarterly* 44, no. 2 (1999): 350–383.

Gabarro, John J., and Linda A. Hill. "Managing Performance." Case 9-496-022. Boston: Harvard Business School, 1995.

Garvin, David A., and Michael A. Roberto. "What You Don't Know About Making Decisions." *Harvard Business Review*, November 2001.

Gentile, Mary C. *Giving Voice to Values*. New Haven, CT: Yale University Press, 2010.

George, Bill, and Doug Baker. *True North Groups: A Powerful Path to Personal and Leadership Development*. San Francisco: Berrett-Koehler Publishers, 2011.

George, Bill, and Peter Sims. *True North: Discover Your Authentic Leadership.* San Francisco: Jossey-Bass, 2007.

Goleman, Daniel. "What Makes a Leader?" *Harvard Business Review*, January 2004.

Greene, Katryn, Valerian J. Derlega, and Alicia Mathews. "Self-Disclosure in Personal Relationships," in *The Cambridge Handbook of Personal Relationships*, ed. Anita L. Vangelisti and Daniel Perlman. Cambridge: Cambridge University Press, 2006.

Groysberg, Boris. *Chasing Stars*. Princeton, NJ: Princeton University Press, 2010.

Hackman, J. Richard. *Leading Teams.* Boston: Harvard Business School Publishing, 2002.

Hackman, J. R., and G. R. Oldham. *Work Redesign*. Reading, MA: Addison-Wesley, 1980.

Heifetz, Ronald A., and Marty Linsky. *Leadership on the Line*. Boston: Harvard Business School Publishing, 2002.

Heineman, Ben W., Jr. "Avoiding Integrity Landmines." *Harvard Business Review*, April 2007.

Hill, Linda A. *Becoming a Manager*. New York: Penguin Books, 1992.

Hill, Linda A. "Note for Analyzing Work Groups." Case 9-496-026. Boston: Harvard Business School, 1998.

Hill, Linda A. "Developing the Star Performer." *Leader to Leader* (Spring 1998): 30–37.

Hill, Linda A. "Becoming the Boss." *Harvard Business Review*, January 2007.

Joyce, William, Nitin Nohria, and Bruce Roberson. *What (Really) Works*. New York: Harper Business Press, 2003.

Kluger, Avraham N., and Angelo DeNisi. "The Effects of Feedback Interventions on Performance: A Historical Review, a Meta-analysis, and a Preliminary Feedback Intervention Theory." *Psychological Bulletin* 119, no. 2 (1996): 254–284.

Kotter, John. "What Leaders Really Do." *Harvard Business Review*, December 2001.

Kram, K. E., and M. C. Higgins. "A New Approach to Mentoring: These Days You Need More Than a Single Person. You Need a Network," *Wall Street Journal*, September 2008.

Kramer, Roderick M. "The Harder They Fall." *Harvard Business Review*, October 2003.

McCall, Morgan W., Jr., and Michael M. Lombardo. "What Makes a Top Executive?" *Psychology Today*, February 1983, 26–31.

McCall, Morgan W., Jr., Michael M. Lombardo, and Ann M. Morrison. *The Lessons of Experience: How Successful Executives Develop on the Job*. New York: Free Press, 1988.

McCauley, Cynthia D., Ellen Van Velsor, and Marian M. Ruderman. "Introduction: Our View of Leadership Development." In *The Center for Creative Leadership Handbook of Leadership Development*. San Francisco: Jossey-Bass, 2004, 1–26.

Nadler, D. *Feedback and Organization Development: Using Data-Based Methods.* Reading, MA: Addison-Wesley, 1977.

Ohlott, Patricia J. "Job Assignments." In *The Center for Creative Leadership's Handbook of Leadership Development*, ed. Cynthia D. McCauley and Ellen Van Velsor. San Francisco: Jossey-Bass, 2004, 151–182.

Roberts, Laura Morgan, Gretchen Spreitzer, Jane Dutton, Robert Quinn, Emily Heapy, and Brianna Barker. "How to Play to Your Strengths." *Harvard Business Review*, January 2005.

Rouiller, Janice T., and I. I. Goldstein. "The relationship between organizational transfer climate and positive transfer of training." *Human Resource Development Quarterly* 4, no. 4 (1993): 377–390.

Schein, Edgar H., and Warren G. Bennis. *Personal and Organizational Change Through Group Methods: The Laboratory Approach.* New York: John Wiley & Sons, 1965.

Thomas, D. A. "The Truth About Mentoring Minorities: Race Matters." *Harvard Business Review*, April 2001.

Tushman, Michael, and David A. Nadler. *Competing by Design: The Power of Organizational Architectures.* New York: Oxford University Press, 1997.

Tushman, Michael L., and Charles A. O'Reilly III. "Managerial Problem Solving: A Congruence Approach." From *Winning Through Innovation.* Boston: Harvard Business School Publishing, 2002.

Welch, Jack. *Straight from the Gut.* New York: Warner Books, 2001.

Yuki, G. *Leadership in Organizations*, 3rd ed. Englewood Cliffs, NJ: Prentice-Hall, 1994.

Zaleznik, Abraham. "Managers and Leaders: Are They Different?" *Harvard Business Review*, March-April 1992.

Notes

Introduction

See Appendix B: A Leadership Reading List.

Chapter One

1. Robert Steven Kaplan and Scott Snook, "The Authentic Leader," course syllabus, Harvard Business School, summer 2014.

See also Michael Beer, Flemming Norregren, et al., *Higher Ambition: How Great Leaders Create Economic and Social Value* (Boston: Harvard Business Review Press, 2011); Daniel Goleman, "What Makes a Leader?" *Harvard Business Review*, January 2004; John Kotter, "What Leaders Really Do," *Harvard Business Review*, December 2001; and Abraham Zaleznik, "Managers and Leaders: Are They Different?" *Harvard Business Review*, March–April 1992.

Chapter Two

1. John J. Gabarro. "Wolfgang Keller at Konigsbrau-TAK (A)." Harvard Business School Case 498-045, December 1997. (Revised October 2008.)

See also Arbinger Institute, *Leadership and Self-Deception* (San Francisco: Berrett-Koehler, 2010); Warren G. Bennis and Robert J. Thomas, "Crucibles of Leadership," *Harvard Business Review*, September 2002; Bill George and Peter Sims, *True North: Discover Your Authentic Leadership* (San Francisco: Jossey-Bass, 2007); and Robert Steven Kaplan and Scott Snook, "The Authentic Leader," course syllabus, Harvard Business School, summer 2014.

Chapter Three

1. Robert Steven Kaplan, *What to Ask the Person in the Mirror: Critical Questions for Becoming a More Effective Leader and Reaching Your Potential*. Boston: Harvard Business Review Press, 2011.

2. Robert Steven Kaplan, *What You're Really Meant to Do: A Road Map for Reaching Your Unique Potential*. Boston: Harvard Business Review Press, 2013.

See also James C. Collins and Jerry Porras, "Building Your Company's Vision," *Harvard Business Review*, September–October 1996; Peter Drucker, *The Essential Drucker* (New York: Harper-Collins, 2001); Mary C. Gentile, *Giving Voice to Values* (New Haven, CT: Yale University Press, 2010); Bill George and Peter Sims, *True North: Discover Your Authentic Leadership* (San Francisco: Jossey-Bass, 2007); Linda A. Hill, "Note for Analyzing Work Groups," Case 9-496-026 (Boston: Harvard Business School, 1998); and Michael L. Tushman and Charles A. O'Reilly III, "Managerial Problem Solving: A Congruence Approach" from *Winning through Innovation: A Practical Guide to Leading Organizational Change and Renewal* (Boston: Harvard Business School Publishing, 2002).

Chapter Four

See Stephen R. Covey, *The 7 Habits of Highly Effective People: Restoring the Character Ethic* (New York: Simon & Schuster, 1989); John J. Gabarro and Linda A. Hill, "Managing Performance," Case 9-496-022 (Boston: Harvard Business School, 1995); David A. Garvin and Michael A. Roberto, "What You Don't Know About Making Decisions," *Harvard Business Review*, November 2001; Bill George and Doug Baker, *True North Groups: A Powerful Path to Personal and Leadership Development* (San Francisco: Berrett-Koehler Publishers, 2011); Bill George and Peter Sims, *True North: Discover Your Authentic Leadership* (San Francisco: Jossey-Bass, 2007), chapter 7; Daniel Goleman, "What Makes a Leader?," *Harvard Business Review*, January 2004; Katryn Greene, Valerian J. Derlega, and Alicia Mathews, "Self-Disclosure in Personal Relationships," in *The Cambridge Handbook of Personal Relationships*, ed. Anita L. Vangelisti and Daniel Perlman (Cambridge: Cambridge University Press, 2006); K. E. Kram and M. C. Higgins, "A New Approach to Mentoring:

These Days You Need More Than a Single Person. You Need a Network," *Wall Street Journal*, September 2008; and Roderick M. Kramer, "The Harder They Fall," *Harvard Business Review*, October 2003.

Chapter Five

1. Bill George and Peter Sims. *True North: Discover Your Authentic Leadership*. San Francisco: Jossey-Bass, 2007.

See also John Paul Eakin, *Living Autobiographically: How We Create Identity in Narrative* (Ithaca, NY: Cornell University Press, 2008); Linda A. Hill, "Becoming the Boss," *Harvard Business Review*, January 2007; Morgan W. McCall, Michael M. Lombardo, and Ann M. Morrison, *The Lessons of Experience: How Successful Executives Develop on the Job* (New York: Free Press, 1998); Cynthia D. McCauley, Ellen Van Velsor, and Marian M. Ruderman "Introduction: Our View of Leadership Development," in *The Center for Creative Leadership Handbook of Leadership Development* (San Francisco: Jossey-Bass, 2004); and Laura Morgan Roberts, Gretchen Spreitzer, Jane Dutton, Robert Quinn, Emily Heapy, and Brianna Barker, "How to Play to Your Strengths," *Harvard Business Review*, January 2005.

Index

Index

Index

Acknowledgments

The ideas and concepts in this book are drawn from a variety of experiences over the past several decades.

I owe a great deal to the numerous mentors, coaches, friends, colleagues, clients, and students whom I have had the privilege to know over these many years. Their wisdom—as well as their generosity in sharing their stories and challenges—has been critical to all that I have learned and forms the basis for much of this book.

I had the good fortune to start my career at Goldman Sachs in the early 1980s. The firm and its leaders instilled in me a business philosophy and approach that I was able to test in a variety of leadership positions over twenty-two years. In addition, our superb clients were generous with their time, wisdom, and ideas—well beyond the requirements of professional relationships. Many of the firm's senior leaders served as role models in helping me develop my management abilities and leadership skills.

I am enormously grateful to my colleagues at Harvard Business School. They gave me the opportunity to join the faculty in 2006 and have helped me become a more effective professor—coaching me to better frame issues, orchestrate effective discussions, and expand my techniques for helping leaders improve their performance.

My fellow professors are generous and rigorous thinkers who are intensely interested in understanding the real world and working to improve it. That's a potent combination, and one that has motivated me to further develop my skills and keep learning. I particularly want to thank my teaching colleagues—Tom DeLong, Robin Ely, Bill George, Ranjay Gulati, Lakshmi Ramarajan, Gautam Mukunda, Josh Margolis, Tsedal Neeley, Nitin Nohria, and Scott Snook—for their advice and guidance.

My classroom experiences have been hugely influential in shaping this book. Since coming to Harvard, I have had the opportunity to teach a significant number of MBAs and executives at all levels, and that has given me exposure to a wide array of leadership, strategy, and competitive challenges and helped me refine my views regarding human potential. My interactions with executives have taught me a great deal and have provided a laboratory for experimenting with various approaches for improving performance and helping individuals achieve their unique potential.

I want to thank *Harvard Business Review* for giving me the opportunity to write articles on leadership and individual potential. Jeff Kehoe and his colleagues at Harvard Business Review Press encouraged me to use those articles as a basis for saying more and worked with me at every step to create this book as well as my previous books.

I could not have written this book without the help of my editor, Jeff Cruikshank. Jeff is an accomplished author in his own right and has served as a superb coach, mentor, and editor. I also want to thank Coleen Kaftan, who read the manuscript and gave me excellent edits and advice. Thank you to Sandy Martin, my fabulous longtime assistant, who puts up with me and makes it possible for me to function efficiently and effectively. Also, Jane Barrett, my assistant at HBS, has been invaluable and outstanding in all that she does. Both Sandy and Jane have helped to keep this project on track over the past year.

Special thanks to Karen Belgiovine, Magda Belgiovine, Michael Diamond, Heather Henriksen, Arlene Kagan, Florence Kaplan, Debra Peltz, Scott Richardson, Mohamed Teffahi, Wendy Winer, David Winer, and Scott Winer for reading and advising me on this manuscript.

Last and most important, I want to thank my parents and family. They have given me love, support, and understanding at every point in my life. Their philosophy, values, and advice echo in the pages of this book.

About the Author

Robert Steven Kaplan is the Martin Marshall Professor of Management Practice and Senior Associate Dean for External Relations at Harvard Business School. He is also cochairman of the Draper Richards Kaplan Foundation, a global venture philanthropy firm. He is the author of several case studies, articles, and two highly regarded books: *What You're Really Meant to Do: A Road Map for Reaching Your Unique Potential* (Harvard Business Review Press, 2013) and *What to Ask the Person in the Mirror: Critical Questions for Becoming a More Effective Leader and Reaching Your Potential* (Harvard Business Review Press, 2011).

Prior to joining Harvard in 2006, Kaplan served as vice chairman of The Goldman Sachs Group, Inc., with global responsibility for the firm's Investment Banking and Investment Management divisions. Previously, he was global cohead of the firm's Investment Banking division. He was also a member of the firm's Management Committee, cochairman of the Partnership Committee, and chairman of the Goldman Sachs Pine Street Leadership Program. During his twenty-three-year career at Goldman Sachs, Kaplan also served in various other capacities, including head of the Corporate Finance department, head of Asia Pacific Investment Banking, and head of the high-yield department in Investment Banking. He became a partner in 1990 and remains a senior director of the firm.

Throughout his career, Kaplan has worked extensively with nonprofit and community organizations. He is cochairman of the board of Project A.L.S., founding chairman of the TEAK Fellowship, cochair of the executive committee of the Harvard Office for Sustainability, and a member of the boards of Harvard Medical School, Harvard Management Company (serving as interim CEO in 2008), and the Ford Foundation. Previously, he was appointed by the governor of Kansas to serve as a board member of the Kansas Health Policy Authority (2006–2010). Kaplan has also served as a member of the Investor Advisory Committee on Financial Markets of the Federal Reserve Bank of New York.

Kaplan is a member of the board of directors of the State Street Corporation, chairman of the Investment Advisory Committee of Google, Inc., and chairman of Indaba Capital Management. Previously, he was a member of the board of directors of Bed Bath & Beyond, Inc. (1994–2009). He also serves as an adviser to a number of companies.

As a professor of management practice at Harvard Business School, Kaplan has taught a variety of leadership courses in the school's MBA program and has also taught many experienced leaders in the school's Executive Education programs. He works extensively with boards and leadership teams of for-profit and not-for-profit organizations in the areas of strategy, leadership, and board effectiveness.

About the Author

Kaplan grew up in Prairie Village, Kansas, and received his BS from the University of Kansas. He earned an MBA from Harvard Business School, where he was a Baker Scholar. Prior to attending business school, he was a certified public accountant at Peat Marwick Mitchell & Company in Kansas City.